GW00359744

THE DIVINE HERO

In over 1,400 books of poetry, essays, plays and short stories, Sri Chinmoy's words have conveyed the richness and diversity of the quest for peace and self-understanding. His published poems number more than 80,000 and his publishers include Simon & Schuster, Harper & Row, Hazelden, Health Communications, Blue Dove Press and Herder & Herder. Sri Chinmoy has offered hundreds of lectures in every state of the United States and throughout the globe at such distinguished universities as Harvard, Yale, Oxford, Cambridge and Tokyo. He lives in Queens, New York.

By the same author

The Wings of Joy

PRAISE FOR SRI CHINMOY

"I am so pleased with all the good work you are doing for world peace and for people in so many countries. May we continue to work together and to share together all for the Glory of God and for the good of man." *Mother Teresa, Nobel Peace Laureate*

"Your loving heart and profound wisdom are a matter of my boundless admiration." *Mikhail Gorbachev, former President of the USSR and Nobel Peace Laureate*

"What you are doing is in the interest of the entire humanity and the world." *Nelson Mandela, Former President of South Africa and Nobel Peace Laureate*

"I would like to hail once again your invaluable contributions to world peace and human togetherness, which are a source of pride and inspiration for political action worldwide. Please accept my sincere thanks for what you are doing for the betterment of mankind." *Javier Perez de Cuellar, former Secretary-General of the United Nations*

"Sri Chinmoy has been a dedicated servant of peace who has been able to bring diverse people together for noble goals. At a time when war continues to rage, violence exists between races, and governments still violate basic human rights, Sri Chinmoy's message of peace is timely and inspirational." *Paul Simon, United States Senator, Illinois*

"Sri Chinmoy is a miraculous model of the abundance in the creative life, and I can only hope that I may someday participate in that cosmic fountain of stillness and profound energy which he inhabits!" *Leonard Bernstein, composer and conductor*

"He has no ego; it is all honest feeling. Sri Chinmoy's music is a magical flow deep down in your heart of hearts." *Addwitiya Roberta Flack, Grammy Award winner*

"By reminding people throughout the world of the importance of striving for peace on a daily basis, the Sri Chinmoy Peace-Blossoms serve a most valuable purpose." *Linus Pauling, Nobel Peace Laureate and Nobel Laureate in Chemistry*

"The word 'peace' is not simply a grouping of letters, but a living entity which must be nurtured if it is to flourish. With every blossom that Sri Chinmoy helps to foster, the dream of world peace becomes a more viable reality." *John Kerry, United States Senator, Massachusetts*

"Sri Chinmoy, you're an inspiration to all of us." *Carl Lewis, eight-time Olympic Gold Medalist*

"Your accomplishments show us that the only limitations to the body and the spirit are the limitations which we place upon ourselves. May the love that you hold for mankind extend from the soul through the body into a real and lasting peace." *Brian Mulroney, former Prime Minister of Canada*

"I believe very much in what you do. I am an admirer of yours. I love what you're doing." *Jesse Owens, four-time Olympic Gold Medalist*

"Sri Chinmoy is a man of peace, a man of faith, and a man of God. He has done so much in the past twenty-five years to make a better world for all of us. The world badly needs more peaceful and loving men like Sri Chinmoy. Sri Chinmoy is doing so much for the world, for people of all faiths, because of his own peace and faith." *Muhammad Ali, three-time World Heavyweight Boxing Champion*

"Thank you very much for all your work." *Archbishop Desmond Tutu, Head, Anglican Church in South Africa*

THE
DIVINE
HERO

Winning in the Battlefield of Life

Sri Chinmoy

Watkins Publishing
London

This edition published in the UK in 2002 by
Watkins Publishing, 20 Bloomsbury Street, London, WC1B 3QA

Cover design by Echelon Design
Front cover artwork © Sri Chinmoy
Back cover photograph © Ranjana Ghose
Typeset by Westkey Ltd, Falmouth, Cornwall
Printed and bound in Great Britain by NFF Production

British Library Cataloguing in Publication data available

Library of Congress Cataloguing in Publication data available

ISBN 1 84293 039 7

Website: www.watkinspublishing.com

Contents

Part One

Heroes of the
Inner World

The Eternal Journey

We are the pilgrims of the Lord Supreme
On the path of Infinity.
At this time we have broken asunder
Obstruction's door.
We have broken asunder the night
Of tenebrous darkness, inconscience
And the eternal, indomitable fear of death.
The Boat of the supernal Light's dawn
Is beckoning us,
And the World-Pilot
Of the hallowed bond of Love divine
Is beckoning us.
The Liberator's Hands are drawing us
To the Ocean of the great Unknown.
Having conquered the life-breath
Of the Land of Immortality,
And carrying aloft the Banner
Of the Lord Supreme,
We shall return –
We, the drops and flames
Of Transformation-Light.

What is a seeker? A seeker of the infinite Light and the eternal Truth has accepted the spiritual life soulfully and consciously. A real seeker, a sincere seeker, is a divine hero, one who meditates on God and whose own consciousness gradually develops to such an extent that he feels God's Presence constantly, everywhere. He feels duty-bound to reveal God's Presence, a Presence that he sees and feels with his own eyes and his own heart.

A real seeker has to fight against teeming darkness to fulfil God's Will here on earth. Otherwise there will always be a yawning gulf between earth and Heaven. This earth of ours must be transformed into Heaven: a place of joy, peace, bliss and delight. We pray and meditate to try to bring light into our system from Above so that we can transform our suffering into joy and our darkness into light.

We must always be brave. Divine courage is our birthright. We are the heroes of the supreme Reality, chosen to struggle with the teeming, brooding and threatening ignorance-night.

> *My Master Lord Supreme,*
> *I love You, I love You only*
> *Because You have given me*
> *Two things absolutely unparalleled:*
> *The map*
> *For the eternal journey*
> *And the courage*
> *For the immortal travelling.*

God And Your Soul

God is playing His divine Game and at each moment He is revealing Himself in us and through us. Who is God? God is our own highest reality. He is one, but He is many. When you look at one of your fingers, you can feel immediately that it is part of your body, because the finger cannot be separated from the body. In the same way, a human being can never be separated from God.

We know that there is something that we call the soul. The soul is the representative of God here on earth, a spark of God. God is in

4

the soul and with the soul, guiding it constantly. God has a particular divine mission to fulfil through your unique soul. To fulfil this mission, He will utilise your soul and no other as His chosen instrument.

The total process of evolution on earth includes the soul as well as the physical form. In the Hindu tradition, *atman* and *paramatman* are the individual soul and the Supreme Self. God comes down into manifestation and takes the form of the individual soul. Then the individual soul in the process of its evolution reaches and becomes the Supreme Self. That is why in India we say *atmanam viddhi*, or "know thyself". If you know yourself, then you know God, because in essence there is no difference between you and God. Self-realisation is God-realisation. In the same vein, all the esoteric traditions have maintained that true knowledge is found within. That is why Jesus said, "The Kingdom of Heaven is within you."

Our philosophy is the acceptance of life for the transformation of life,
And also for the manifestation of God's Light here on earth,
At God's choice Hour, in God's own Way.

The Soul: God's Representative

Right now when we think of ourselves, we think of our body and not of our soul. Unfortunately, we identify ourselves all the time with our lowest part. Our being is like a house that belongs to us. We do not use the third floor at all, but spend most of our time in the basement or on the first floor. Since we spend most of our time there, we feel the basement is our reality. The third floor is also ours, if only we can find our way there.

The soul fights against doubt, obscurity, ignorance, imperfection, limitations, worries and so forth. It tries to reveal its own inner divinity and establish the divine Truth on earth according to its capacity. The soul is uncovering what it has always known, but while it is uncovering, it is growing and enriching itself by taking into itself the divine essence of its earthly experiences. Meanwhile, the physical consciousness is becoming more and more conscious of the soul's unlimited divine capacity.

In God's cosmic Drama,
Divinity employs the soul
To bring the message of Light and Delight
Down into the very heart
Of the earth-consciousness.

The Heart: Doorway To The Soul

Next to the soul in purity and divinity is the heart. I am not speaking of the physical heart, which is just another organ. I am speaking of the spiritual heart. The spiritual heart is located in the centre of your chest, in the centre of your existence. The consciousness of the soul pervades the whole body, but most of the time the soul chooses to stay inside the heart. If you can concentrate on the heart, then you are knocking at the door of the soul, which is the door of the Supreme.

The heart is most important in your spiritual discipline, because the heart represents identification. If you want to grow into something, then you have to identify yourself with it. You look at a flower and you appreciate its beauty and fragrance. Then you try to grow into the very same consciousness that the flower embodies, its purity and beauty. In the spiritual life also, when we enter into the heart, we identify immediately with its light, peace, power and bliss. On the strength of our identification, we grow into divine reality.

6

If we want to reach the Highest as soon as possible, then the path ofthe heart must be followed so that the light of our soul can come to the fore.

> *You will see your heart's inner bird*
> *Singing and soaring*
> *Beyond your expectation-summit,*
> *If you can allow*
> *Your heart's morning star*
> *To beckon your outer life.*

The Mind: Turmoil-Surface, Tranquillity-Depths

The mind has, up until now, been humanity's greatest achievement. With its help, science and our physical world have progressed to an enormous extent. However, the reasoning mind is really an obstacle for a spiritual aspirant. The mind is fond of accumulating information, but information is not going to give us an iota of inner wisdom.

Once we are aware that the mind is not being utilised properly, but that it can be used for the service of the Divine, then we have come one step forward. The next step is to know what is hidden inside the mind – what capacities, possibilities and potentialities the mind already embodies. The surface of the ocean is all turmoil, but when we observe the bottom of the ocean, it is all peace and tranquillity. Similarly, the mind is full of turmoil, tension and obscurity on the surface, but when we go deep inside the mind, we find the higher mind, far beyond the domain of doubt. Right now we do not really know Infinity, Eternity and Immortality. These are vague terms that the physical mind cannot grasp. But if we enter into the higher mind, then we see these things as the real Reality.

7

The prayer that soars above
Unlocks the perfection-door for you.
The mind that dives within
Shows you the satisfaction-room.

The Vital: Seat Of The Emotions

When I use the word "vital", I refer to the dynamic, emotional part of our nature – to an energy that we can use or misuse, that we can use in a human way or a divine way.

The human vital comprises such emotions as ordinary joy, sorrow, anger and excitement. Emotion, by itself, is not bad unless we misuse it. When we misuse it, we try to possess either an object or an individual or the whole world. In this way the human vital binds and limits us, and finally drains our physical and mental energy.

But the divine vital says, "I know how to spread my love-wings. Why? Because that is the only way I can have satisfaction." Divine emotion expands our consciousness and is always welcome. It is the expression of our inner aspiration. It lifts us up into the inner sky.

If you want to make something happen
In your life,
Then your vital must play the role
Of a revolutionary pioneer.

The Body: Home Of The Soul

The soul, which is a conscious, divine portion of God, has to live inside the physical body in order to make progress. Inside a church is the altar. Similarly, the body is a temple, and inside the temple is the shrine, the soul.

The physical as such is very limited. By nature, it is lethargic; it does not want to budge an inch. The Light is descending, descending, but the physical is the lowest part of the being, and here the Light finds it extremely difficult to operate. The physical is the last place to receive Light, but when a person begins to aspire consciously, his entire being gradually starts to aspire. His soul aspires, his heart aspires, his mind aspires, his vital aspires and finally his body aspires. When the physical in the aspirant starts to become one with the soul's inspiration and aspiration, then God's Light can find a fit receptacle in him.

My awakened body
Is walking from glory to glory.
My transformed vital
Is marching from glory to glory.
My illumined mind
Is running from glory to glory.
My liberated heart
Is flying from glory to glory.
My fulfilled soul
Is dancing from glory to glory.

The Life of a Divine Hero

O voyager of time,
Onward you proceed
And offer to the world
Your achievement-light.
Much have you to discover,
Much have you to offer,
O voyager of time.

The spiritual life is the life of a hero. You have to take the side of the divine forces all the time. These divine forces are constantly trying to save and illumine you. In each human being there is a constant battle going on between the divine and undivine. The hostile forces attack us because, deep inside our being, our consecration to God, the Supreme, is not yet complete.

There are many heroes of the inner world, but the main heroes are simplicity, sincerity, purity, aspiration, dedication and surrender. These divine heroes help the seeker discover God and help him overcome bondage-night and ignorance-day. Their supreme commander is faith. Divine love and sincere gratitude support these heroes.

Simplicity shortens the road that leads to God-discovery. Sincerity expedites the journey. Purity feeds the seeker and the journey together. Aspiration loves the journey. Dedication enjoys the journey. And surrender completes the journey.

Simplicity is a very simple word, but it embodies tremendous power. When we enter into the spiritual life, we value this most significant achievement. We have countless desires. But from our list, if we can take out one desire, then to that extent our life becomes simple. When it becomes simple, an iota of peace dawns in our mental firmament. Each time we become simple, simpler, simplest, our desire-life becomes short, shorter, shortest. Then we enjoy peace of mind; we enjoy light and delight.

Sincerity is our peerless achievement. If we can become sincere, then we can run the fastest in our spiritual life. When we make friends with insincerity, at every moment we have to justify our insincere life. Once we tell a lie, we have to tell twenty more lies in order to justify that particular lie. And each time we tell a lie, we add a heavy burden to our shoulders. How can we run the fastest when there is a heavy load on our shoulders? But when we are sincere, we accelerate our progress; we run the fastest, like a deer.

Purity is of paramount importance in the spiritual life. Purity means the power of receptivity. When our heart is inundated with purity, we feel that our inner receptacle has become large, larger, largest. Peace, light and bliss enter into that vessel from Above. And inside the vessel we see our divine qualities sporting, dancing and fulfilling their reality's light and delight. Purity is receptivity's capacity. When we are pure, immediately our self-expansion, our divine reality, looms large.

Aspiration, dedication and surrender. Aspiration is our journey's start. Aspiration is the flow of our journey, the continuous, endless journey itself. Aspiration is an inner cry. This cry liberates us from the meshes of ignorance. This cry eventually makes us one with the Eternal, the Infinite and the Immortal. When we aspire, we feel that deep within us there is a higher reality that we, unfortunately, cannot right now claim as our very own. But there comes a time when, on the strength of our own aspiration, we can claim this reality – our own highest, supernal Reality – as our own, very own. Each time we aspire, we bring to the fore our own hidden, divine, immortal Reality.

Dedication. When we dedicate ourselves to a cause, we expand our own reality-existence. This dedication is not done under any compulsion. Responsibility has not been thrust upon us. It is we who want to expand our reality, so we adopt the right approach and try to expand ourselves through dedication. One becomes many; again, many become one. As individuals, when we dedicate ourselves devotedly, soulfully and unconditionally, we grow into the many. And when we do this as a collective body, we become one. It is through dedication that we become many and that we become one. When we become one, we fulfil God as Infinity's Silence, birthless and deathless Silence. When we become many, we fulfil God as the eternal, infinite sound, birthless and deathless sound. Finally, we fulfil God the soundless Sound.

Surrender. Surrender completes the journey. This surrender is our conscious awareness of our highest Reality. It is not the surrender of a slave; it is the surrender of the finite in us to the Infinite in us. The unlit, obscure, impure existence of ours is surrendering to the illumined, pure and perfect existence of our own Reality-Height. We are not surrendering to a second or third person. We are surrendering to the Divine within us, to the Infinite within us, to the Immortal within us. Surrender here is our conscious and constant expansion, illumination, liberation and perfection. Each time we surrender our earth-bound existence to our Heaven-free life, we enjoy nectar, divine bliss.

When the seeker establishes his body's reality-oneness with the Will of the Supreme, he becomes the simplicity-hero. When the seeker establishes his mind's reality-oneness with the Will of the Supreme, he becomes a sincerity-hero. When the seeker establishes his vital's reality-oneness with the Will of the Supreme, he becomes a purity-hero. When the seeker establishes his heart's reality-oneness with the Will of the Supreme, he becomes an aspiration-hero. The same seeker, in the course of time, when he establishes his life's reality-oneness with the Will of the Supreme, becomes a dedication-hero. Finally, when the seeker consciously, devotedly, untiringly, unreservedly and unconditionally establishes his soul's oneness-reality with the Will of the Absolute Supreme, he becomes a surrender-hero. The seeker is able to accomplish all this with his heart of love and his life of gratitude.

> *Every seeker must know*
> *That everything that is good*
> *And divine in him*
> *Will come to the fore to love God,*
> *Realise God and manifest God*
> *On earth.*

The Undivine Forces

As there are many divine forces of the inner world, even so there are many undivine ones. The main undivine forces, or weaknesses, are disobedience, insecurity, fear, doubt, lethargy and self-indulgence.

Disobedience is the worst weakness in the seeker's life. A seeker may listen to the inner dictates quite often. But if one day he disobeys the inner command, then he is bound to notice a hole in the life-boat which is destined to take him to the Golden Shore of the Beyond. His life-boat has sprung a leak. Gradually the hole will become large, larger, largest, and his spiritual boat will capsize and sink. But if he is obedient, then his life-boat will sail fast, faster, fastest towards the destined Goal, the Goal of the highest ever-transcending Beyond.

Insecurity starts in the mind, but the mind is not aware of insecurity at the beginning. From the mind it enters into the vital, and finally it comes to the physical consciousness. At that time we are fully aware of the presence of insecurity. Insecurity is a poisonous disease. If we do not get rid of it, this poison spreads and eventually destroys the whole system.

Fear is worse. Fear of the unknown, not to speak of fear of the unknowable, is a fatal disease in the seeker's life. The seeker is afraid of everything that is not in his domain. He fears others, he fears the unknown, he fears the Vast; finally he becomes afraid of himself. At every moment he is afraid of his own possessions, not to speak of others' achievements or realities.

Then comes doubt. Doubt is an almost incurable disease in us. If we judge others with our unlit human mind, with the intellectual mind, with the sophisticated mind, the people whom we judge do not lose an iota of their achievement, of their reality. But we lose. How do we lose? When we start doubting others, we lose something of our own existence to the outer world; something of our own reality goes. First we doubt someone and immediately afterwards we try to see whether we are correct in doubting that person. Then we begin to judge and doubt ourselves. When we doubt ourselves, we lose everything.

We cannot judge others. We do not know their heights; we do not know their depths. We do not know what is actually happening inside the hearts of others. It is the cosmic Will that is operating in and through each and every individual. We are in no position to judge others. Each person is guided, moulded and shaped by the Will of the unseen Hand.

We should follow the path of faith. Faith is the commander in us. Faith tells us of the existence of Reality and Truth in us, for us. Then faith tells us that we not only embody the Truth, eternal Truth, infinite Truth, but we are this transcendental Truth, this universal Truth ourselves.

Then comes lethargy. When the Hour of God strikes, if we do not respond, then we cannot start our journey. The road is long, very long. When the Hour strikes, owing to lethargy, if we do not respond

14

to the call of the Hour, we unconsciously lengthen our road. The mind becomes totally immersed in ignorance and feels that the road is longer than the longest.

Another undivine force is self-indulgence. If we enter into the world of self-indulgence, then instead of running forward, we run backward. And each time we run backward, we again make friends with our old friend, doubt.

A spiritual seeker has to be aware of these undivine forces: disobedience, insecurity, fear, doubt, lethargy and self-indulgence. The divine heroes have only one thing to tell us: accept light and reject night. Acceptance of light is the only thing that is needed. Night is the ignorance within us. Ignorance-night binds our body, blinds our eyes, stabs our heart. When we are attacked by the undivine forces, the divine heroes come to our rescue and offer us perfection-light. As the representative of the Supreme, this perfection-light first liberates us, then illumines us and grants us vision. It grants vision to our eyes and then immortalises our heart. This is what perfection-light does for us.

Now that I have liberated myself
From my undisciplined days and nights,
My heart is sweetly drawn
To my Lord Beloved Supreme.

Inner Awareness, Outer Action

There are divine heroes of the outer world as well as of the inner world. The outer heroes are our divine personality and divine individuality, which say, "I am of God and I am for God." The inner heroes become one with God's Will, and in this way they feel that they are establishing God, the eternal Truth and Light, in the inner world.

The outer heroes strive for God's Victory on earth at every moment in the outer world. The outer heroes want to establish the Kingdom of Heaven on earth. They want to see the Infinite in the finite.

But the inner heroes see that Infinity is already there in the finite. They see that the finite does not have the vision to see the Infinite, whereas the Infinite can envision its own presence in the finite itself. The inner heroes are aware of what they eternally are, whereas the outer heroes are not. Therefore, they do something in order to become. The inner heroes feel that they do not have to become; they already are.

But there comes a time when the inner and outer heroes become one, inseparably one. The inner heroes bring to the outer heroes the message of realisation: realisation of the infinite Truth, eternal Light and immortal Delight. And the outer heroes try to manifest the divine realities, the divine treasures that are offered to them by the inner heroes. The inner heroes bring these realities to the earth-arena. The outer heroes manifest these realities in the earth-arena. This way both the inner heroes and the outer heroes complete the cosmic Lila, the divine Game.

There is only one ultimate solution:
Love God the Creator
And serve God the creation.

The Attitude Of A Divine Hero

Everyone needs victory. There are two kinds of victory. One is transient, transitory, like a mound of sand. The other is eternal, everlasting. When we gain victory by force, this victory does not last. But when we gain victory as the result of our soul's oneness with the Supreme and our soul's delight, this victory lasts for good.

A man who is by nature cowardly wants to conquer fear. If he can conquer fear, he feels that he will become his true self, his fearless divine self. A poor man wants to be rich; he wants to become a multimillionaire. By amassing money, he feels that he will gain victory over his poverty. A spiritual man wants to conquer ignorance, limitation, bondage and death. By conquering ignorance, he feels that he can become one with Immortality.

You should always have the attitude of a divine hero. A divine hero is a spiritual person who will work for the divine manifestation here on earth – who will act for the sake of the Divine, the Supreme. If we are frightened when a problem arises, then we cannot be chosen instruments of the Divine, of the Supreme. Life has to be accepted.

Granted, the world is all imperfection. We face problems every day. Moreover, the more spiritually advanced a person is, the greater is his suffering, due to the present conditions of the world. The world embodies divinity, but we deny even this simple truth. We have to feel the embodiment of the ultimate Truth in this world of ours, and then to reveal and manifest that Truth with our dynamic meditation, conscious aspiration and sincere dedication.

> *If seeing is believing,*
> *Then at every moment*
> *Keep your heart's eye*
> *Wide open*
> *And see the divine reality*
> *In everything.*

Thoughts

There are various kinds of undivine forces that have the form of thoughts. The thoughts that we have to control are the thoughts that are not productive, the thoughts that are damaging or negative. These thoughts can come from outside us and enter in, or they may already be inside us and merely come forward.

The thoughts that come from outside are easier to control than those that are already inside. If an undivine thought comes from outside, we have to make ourselves feel consciously that we have a shield all around us or right in front of us as a protection.

The thoughts that are already inside us creating problems are more difficult to throw out, but we can do it through an extension of our consciousness. What we have to do is use our imagination to extend our physical consciousness, as we extend an elastic band, until we feel that our whole body is extended to Infinity and has become just a white sheet of infinitely extended consciousness.

Each moment we are thinking either good thoughts or bad thoughts; divine thoughts or undivine thoughts. If we constantly harbour good thoughts, pure thoughts, divine thoughts, then the negative forces can never stay in us, because they know well that, the moment they enter, they will be suffocated. There is no room left for them.

> When each and every thought of mine
> I place at the Feet
> Of my Lord Beloved Supreme,
> I see myself sailing
> With the prayerful, soulful
> And fruitful peace-wind
> At my back.

The Greatest Duty

The source of these negative forces inside us is ignorance. Ignorance is the root of all our problems. We can even think of evil or sin as ignorance. Eventually ignorance will be transformed into knowledge.

When a negative force speaks from inside you, it will say, "You cannot be God's chosen child. Impossible! You have done millions of things wrong." The negative force will tell you that you cannot become the perfect instrument of God and that you cannot grow into His very image.

Immediately you have to say, "All right, I have done millions of things wrong, but that is none of your business. I am not taking shelter from you. I am not going to be under your protection, your wings. I am under the protection of the omniscient and omnipotent Supreme."

Immediately the positive forces will tell you, "Yes, you already are an instrument, a chosen instrument of God. You are growing into the very image of God because God Himself is evolving in and through you. Unfortunately, you are not aware of it. That is why you are suffering."

In order to achieve victory, we must have patience, we must have endurance and, most important, we must have will-power. If there is no will-power, then it is useless to fight against anything or try to transform anything. What we need most is will-power. This will-power is the conviction of our soul. It is our soul's will and determination.

What is the greatest duty in human life? Self-conquest, the conquest of one's own self. Who actually wins the victory when we conquer the lowest in ourselves? It is not us, but God the Supreme within us, who wins the victory.

I am very happy
Because I have conquered myself
And not the world.
I am very happy
Because I have loved the world
And not myself.

I am very happy
Because I have not surrendered
Either to the world or to myself.

Whose Victory Is It?

There is a significant story from India's ancient text the *Upanishads*. Once the cosmic gods won a victory over the demons and, naturally, their pride knew no bounds. They thought that they were fully responsible for their victory. They felt that it was their own strength and power that enabled them to defeat the demons. The Absolute Brahman wanted to smash their pride. He disguised Himself as a brahmin, an old man, an invalid, and approached the cosmic gods. They were a bit surprised and asked him, "What do you want?"

He said, "I do not want anything from you. I just want to know what you are boasting of."

They said, "We have just won a victory over the demons with our strength and valour, so we are rejoicing."

The old man said, "Well, just do me a favour. I am leaving a piece of straw right in front of you. I wish one of you could blow it away or do something with it." The wind god came and tried to blow away the straw, but the straw did not budge an inch. Then the fire god, Agni, came and tried to burn the straw; but alas, fire could not devour it. Like this, it went on and on.

Finally, Indra, Lord of the gods, came in. When he came, the brahmin disappeared and in his place there was a goddess in a column of light. Indra asked the goddess about the mystery of this brahmin. The goddess said, "It was not a brahmin, it was the Absolute Brahman who wanted to show you the Truth. It was with His strength that you conquered the demons. You have no power. It was the Brahman Absolute who wanted to humble your pride and teach you that it was not your strength that won the victory, but His Strength."

Whenever we achieve success or attain to some perfection, we must feel that it is the divine power that has enabled us to do so. We need the help, we need the blessings of the Supreme. The Supreme wants us to be freed from the fetters of our ignorance. The day we are freed from ignorance, His joy will know no bounds. Right now, we have veiled the divinity inside us. With the blessings of the Supreme and the guidance and loving concern of a spiritual Teacher, the pilot of our life-boat, we can easily unveil the divinity within us. At the same time, we can swim across the ocean of ignorance and enter into the ocean of Light. When we enter into the ocean of Light, what we see and feel and become is victory. And whose victory is it? It is the Victory of the Supreme.

Do the right thing.
Be the right person.
Lo, God is coming
To garland
Your self-giving life.

Part Two

The Divine Heroes

Simplicity

Be simple, be sincere,
Be pure and be humble.
Go back,
Go back once more
To the basics of your inner life.

To have simplicity is to run towards God without darkness, worries or impurity. In the spiritual life the higher we go, the deeper we go, the farther we go, the more we will see that Reality is only the song of simplicity and nothing else. God is always simple, but we think of Him as complex. The entire cosmic Game is extremely simple, but we look at it from a different angle in an obscure way.

For us, everything is complex because we always use the mind. We do not want to walk along a straight line. If a path is simple and straight, we feel that it has no value. Unless we zigzag in a serpentine way, we get no joy. Just because we value complexity, we do not take the sunlit path – the simple, straight path. Right from the beginning of our lives we become accustomed to doing things in a very complicated way, so simplicity is most difficult for us.

When a child is born, the mother spends a lot of money on buying him the most beautiful and expensive clothes. She wants to show that she is richer than her neighbours. The child would be equally happy with simple clothes, but right from the beginning he is taught that simple things are not good. So naturally when the child grows up, he does not care for simplicity. A simple person will have only what he needs, and he will know the difference between what he needs and what he wants. But we tend to feel that whatever we want, we desperately need. We are trying to possess the world. But before we possess the world, to our wide surprise we see that the world has already possessed us.

> *This world has nothing for you.*
> *Suddenly, one day you will start going*
> *Your own way.*
> *Your way, too, will have nothing*
> *For you.*
> *Eventually you will start going God's Way,*
> *For that is the only Way.*

The Mango Garden

If we use the mind, we will feel that nothing is as difficult or complicated as spirituality. But if we really want to follow the spiritual life, if we use the heart as our instrument, then nothing can be more simple. When the heart wants to identify itself with something or someone, it uses the feeling of love and oneness. But when the mind wants to see something, it tries to delay and separate. The mind unconsciously gets pleasure in things that are complicated and confused, but the heart gets joy in things that are simple.

If a friend of yours comes and gives you a most delicious mango, will you immediately eat the mango? Will you instead ask him questions – where he got it, how much it cost, was it imported? In the spiritual life there are two types of seekers. One type will just see the reality and immediately try to become the reality. The other type will immediately begin to question, examine and doubt the reality.

Suppose both of these seekers are hungry and you take them into a mango garden where there are many mangoes. The first kind of seeker will say, "All right, since there are many mangoes, I will now be able to eat." But the second type of seeker will say, "I wonder how many mangoes are here," and start counting them. Then he will want to know which one is the best, so he will start examining all the mangoes to decide which one he should take. While he is wasting his time, the first seeker will take a mango and just eat it, and he will be satisfied.

If we use the mind, we will always try to analyse everything and we will never experience the reality. If we start counting all the mangoes, perhaps we will never begin eating. Or after a while we may get disgusted and say, "Who wants to know?" During the time we spend in counting we lose our spontaneous inner joy. But if we use the heart, we will immediately take the thing we want.

The fulfilment of the mind
Has been the hope
Of the past few centuries.
Now the fulfilment of the heart
Will be the hope
Of the next generation
And of all generations to come.
Indeed, this will be a unique contribution
Of the twenty-first century to humanity.

A Child's Simplicity-Heart

If somebody is inwardly spiritual, he is like a beautiful and simple child. A child's heart is all simplicity. But when this child develops the mind and lives in the mind, then world-confusion enters into him. At that time fear, doubt, anxiety, jealousy and many other undivine forces weigh him down, so naturally he cannot run fast.

Complexity is in the mind and not in the heart. We need the heart of a child in order to run the fastest.

Mere years do not make a person old. Somebody who is sixty or seventy years of age may have the enthusiasm, inner joy and inspiration of a child. Again, there will be people who are seventeen, eighteen or nineteen years old who have no aspiration, no inspiration, no dynamism. If a person of nineteen does not have the capacity to draw something from or offer something to the world, if he does not care for the world and feels that he does not need anything from the world, then he is old in spirit. On the other hand, if somebody of ninety-nine wants to learn the inner language – the language of divine love, peace, wisdom and light – then he is a child in spirit. In the spiritual life we are not concerned with earthly years but with an individual's inner eagerness to do something and to become something – to become a child of God.

If you really want to become a child, then you have to feel that there is always something to learn and that God is there to teach you. In the spiritual life you are learning something every day, every hour, every minute, every second from our divine Father. If you constantly have the feeling that you are learning in the inner world, there is no end to the God-divinity that you can receive and achieve.

A God-blossoming heart
Remains
Eternally young.

God's Concern

Because a child lives in the heart, he always feels that his mother or his father will take care of him. All the time he feels that there is protection, there is guidance, there is assistance. So naturally he has confidence in his life. Because he is always in the heart, he feels that there is no need which his parents will not fulfil. If he lived in the mind, he would immediately think, "Oh, perhaps my father will not be able to do this. Perhaps my mother will not be there to help me." Then he would become fearful, doubtful and anxious. But a child does not live in the mind. Similarly, if you want to have a childlike spirit, no matter how old you are, you have to feel that there is Someone with infinitely more wisdom-light who is constantly thinking of you, guiding you and protecting you, and that this Person is God.

Imagine for a moment that you are a small child. Your mother is showing you all her affection. She shows her concern for you day in and day out. But out of twenty-four hours, your mother can offer you only two or three hours of conscious concern. When you are sick, perhaps she will offer her concern for fifteen or sixteen or twenty-four hours. But when you are well, she has to do quite a few things apart from taking care of you, even though you are her dearest.

God's Concern is different. His Concern started from the very beginning and it will remain the same forever. The moment He created you, His Concern started, and this Concern will last for Eternity. Where does it come from? The source of God's Concern is His Oneness.

When something is wrong with a family member, you show that person concern because of your oneness. There are many who are suffering whom you do not know. And even if you do know them, you are not going to offer your concern. Why? Because you are not completely identified with them. But you do feel oneness with your family. Again, when your finger is hurt, immediately you are concerned for your finger. Why? Because you are one with your finger. Similarly, God is all Concern because He is one with everything and everyone. Because of His all-pervading Oneness, He has to offer His Concern. You have to know that God loves you infinitely more than your own mother loves you. His Love lasts for Eternity.

You can forget everything
If you want to.
But do not forget one thing:
You are God's child,
God's very, very own.

The Desire-Life And The Simplicity-Life

Each seeker has two individuals inside: one is desiring, the other is aspiring. Because we have accepted the spiritual life, we have to ask ourselves whether desire satisfies us and fulfils us or not. In our inner being we will feel that it does neither. Before we actually desire, we have in mind the object or fruit of our desire, and we think that when we attain that object, we will be happy. Unfortunately what we eventually get is frustration. Each time we fulfil one desire, we succumb to more desires. But even the fulfilment of the desire itself does not give us satisfaction. On the contrary, it increases our greed, our dissatisfaction with what we see, what we feel and what we are growing into.

Desires, for a seeker, have to be transformed into the life of aspiration. They have to be illumined. If you feel that once a particular desire is fulfilled, you will no longer enter into the world of desire, that you will immediately enter the world of aspiration, you are mistaken. It is not possible. The life of desire is a tempting life. You cannot say that once twenty desires are fulfilled, you will enter into the spiritual life. At that time the twenty-first desire will come to claim you. Once you enter the spiritual life, you have to feel that each desire has to be offered to the Lord for its transformation, for its illumination.

My life
Is not a passing pleasure.
It is a lasting treasure
Of God.

Material Success Or Spiritual Success

If you want God, you have to lead a simple life. There are only twenty-four hours in the day, and when they are gone, they do not come back again. If you waste an hour, then it is lost to you forever. You will not be able to retrieve it. You have to decide what you will use each fleeting moment for: for worldly pleasure or for God. If you feel that your first and foremost necessity is God, then if you simplify your life, you will not be distracted or tempted.

There are many things we do here on earth that are unnecessary. There are many things we own that are superfluous. If we have one car, we want to have two cars. If we have one house, we want to have two houses. We try constantly to increase our material possessions instead of existing with the minimal things we need to live here on earth. But we have to know what we really want. If we want to be spiritual, then naturally we have to spend most of our time in spiritual pursuits.

You may feel that when your material life is fully secure and you have achieved some material success, when you have attained some sense of outer joy or perfection, then it will become easier for you to enter into the spiritual life. Now, there is nothing wrong with this. But most seekers have found that what they have achieved on the physical, outer plane is not an asset or additional help to their spiritual life. If you are well established in the outer life, if you are secure and have achieved some measure of success, that is wonderful. But if you feel that these outer achievements will expedite your spiritual progress, that is not true in most cases. On the contrary, usually it will be the other way around. Many people have achieved earthly success. But often their spiritual life will be more difficult, because ego, pride and a sense of self-sufficiency may stand in the way of materially successful people.

Real spiritual success is the conscious surrender of our will to the Will of the Almighty. There is nothing wrong if material success and spiritual success go together, provided we are ready to sacrifice everything for spiritual success. But what usually happens is just the opposite. When material success begins to make demands on us, we sacrifice our spiritual life to the demands of the material life.

> *The sweetest and the richest*
> *Of all occupations*
> *Is when I think of God*
> *And I feel God*
> *As my Eternity's own,*
> *Very own.*

Matter And Spirit

We do not have to abandon the outer life. We have only to go deep within. Then we have to see how much of the outer life is really necessary in order to lead a spiritual life. How we use the material life is what is of paramount importance. Matter, as such, has not done anything wrong to God; it is not undivine. It is we who use material things in a wrong way. We must enter into the material life with our soul's light. We can use a knife to stab someone or we can use it to cut a fruit to share with others. With fire we can cook and with fire we can also burn ourselves or set fire to someone's house.

We have to feel that matter and spirit go together. Matter has to be the conscious expression of spirit. There is an inner reality, there is an infinite Truth that wants to express itself in and through matter. Matter is asleep, and it has to be aroused. The material life has to be guided and moulded by the spirit. But first we have to understand what the material life is for. If by material life we mean lower vital enjoyment and the fulfilment of gross desires, then it is useless to try to accept the spiritual life simultaneously. But if the material life means the life of expansion – the expansion of the heart, the expansion of love – then matter and spirit can easily go together. The true material life is not just eating, sleeping and drinking. The material life is a significant life.

But when it is a matter of choosing between the outer and inner life, we have to pay more attention to the inner life. Then we will have solid joy, peace, love and power, and whatever is unnecessary in the outer life we can transform. There are things that are of paramount importance in the outer life that we must accept. But things which have to be given up in the outer life we shall give up. We have to simplify our life. Inside simplicity is purity; inside purity is divinity.

If we are absolutely dedicated
To the divine cause,
And if we can listen to the dictates
Of our inner being
At every moment,
Our inner being will create
Outer circumstances that will help us
In our spiritual life.

33

What Should We Renounce?

Certainly we have to renounce in the spiritual life. But we are not going to renounce individuals, we are going to renounce qualities – the qualities which stand in the way of our union with the Divine. We are going to renounce doubt, imperfection, ignorance and death. When we enter into the spiritual life, we get the opportunity to renounce, or rather, to transform these things. When we speak of renouncing or transforming something, we immediately think of ignorance. Truly, ignorance is the one thing that we have to transform in our spiritual life.

From the strict spiritual point of view, so-called earthly renunciation is not necessary for an aspirant. If renunciation means leaving one's family, not caring for society or humanity, then I wish to say that no matter what we renounce today, there will be something else to stand in our way tomorrow. Today our family is the obstacle; tomorrow it will be our friends and relatives; the day after tomorrow it will be our country and the day after that, the world. There is no end to this kind of renunciation.

Asceticism is not necessary for God-realisation. In order to realise God, I do not have to torture my being. If I cut off my arms and run toward my Father and say, "Father, look, just for You I have cut off my arms," God will not be pleased. Too much asceticism, or torturing the body in the name of discipline, is not good. Discipline is necessary but, like anything else, when you go to the extreme, it is very bad. We should adopt the middle path, like the Buddha. We should not be over-indulgent and, at the same time, we should not be overly strict with our physical consciousness.

It is the same with the monastic life. Perhaps when we are living a very materialistic life and wish to change, then it would be good to lead a monastic life for a very brief period, but that is all. We must strike a balance; we need not build a Taj Mahal in order to meditate in a palace every day, but we must not go to a cave either. Those days are gone.

> Your daily life is peopled with
> Seekers and non-seekers,
> God-doubters and God-believers.
> Your eye of concern
> Encompasses them
> And your heart of love
> Teaches them.

The Inner Cry

In order to realise God, what is necessary is the inner cry, and this inner cry we can have even when we are walking along the street. It is a mistake to feel that we will feel the inner cry only if we are at the top of the Himalayas. Even there, our minds will roam and we will think of our friends, our relatives and our enemies. Again, here in the world, in the hustle and bustle of life, we can easily think of God. As long as our activities are dedicated to God, God-realisation can take place, must take place, and will take place here on earth in the midst of multifarious activities.

If a spiritual Master has an ashram and we go there to meditate, that is wonderful. But if all seekers renounce the world and enter into monasteries or secluded places to meditate, then who is going to transform the face of the world? In the modern world, we have to play the role of heroes, divine heroes. If somebody says he is going to renounce the world in order to realise God, then I wish to say that he is mistaken. By leaving everyone, whom are we accepting? God? No! God is in each human soul. Today we will renounce the world and tomorrow we will find that the God we are seeking is nowhere else. God is in the world itself.

You can shorten the road
To Eternity,
If you can take everything
As divine
And every man
As a truth-seeker
And a God-lover.

Sincerity

All I need to know
Is if my heart's cry for God
Is completely genuine.

We always know whether we are sincere or not. Sincerity is not something that we have to be taught; it comes from deep within. When something comes to the fore from the inmost recesses of our heart, we are bound to be sincere. This is not true in the case of the mind. The mind is consciously negating things. One moment we think that something is true and we are ready to fight for it, and the next moment we discover that it is absolutely false.

If our focus of concentration is in our heart, then easily we will be able to feel that what is coming to the fore from the inmost recesses of our heart is all sincerity. Inside the heart is the soul. The soul cannot be anything else but the flood of sincerity. More than that, it is the flood of spirituality. Through the heart, the soul speaks most powerfully and convincingly. If we spend more time in our heart than in our mind, we are bound to know what sincerity is.

Rewarded For His Sincerity

Once in a small village there was a shortage of water, because there had been no rain for a long time. The villagers were suffering from lack of water. The king came to know of it, and he ordered his minister to create a pond. The minister then ordered his assistant to make the pond. The assistant in turn asked his assistant, and that assistant asked his own assistant. Finally, one of the workers in the village was ordered to dig a pond and then there was plenty of water.

The king wanted to see if the pond was in good condition and if it was full of water. Others all followed him to see the pond. The king was very, very pleased inwardly, but outwardly he said, "This is a very bad job. This pond is not good at all." He showed great displeasure. He said, "The water will one day run out of the pond." So many defects the king found!

Then the king became angry with his minister. He said, "Now, Minister, tell me what happened. I gave you a job, and you did not do it satisfactorily."

The minister's assistant pointed to his own assistant and said, "I asked him to do it because I was very busy. I have so much to do."

Like that it went on and on. Everybody was blaming his subordinate in turn. Finally the king came to know which fellow had actually dug the pond. This poor village worker came before the king shaking. The king asked him abruptly, "Did you dig this pond?"

The poor man said, "Yes, my boss asked me to do it. He gave me specific instructions. I did it, and my boss was satisfied."

The king said, "But I am not satisfied. I am the king. Whether or not your boss is satisfied is irrelevant. I am the one you must satisfy."

The man said, "Your Majesty, if you are not fully satisfied with my work, then please punish me in whichever way you want to punish me."

Then the king started laughing. After a few moments, he took out a bag containing a thousand rupees and gave it to the man. The man was astonished. He said, "You were mad at me. Now you are giving me money. I do not understand this at all."

The king said, "No, I am very, very pleased with you. You are an excellent worker. But I wanted to find out who was actually responsible for digging the pond. Because I found fault with them and scolded them, the others all said that they were not responsible. Each one, in turn, passed the responsibility to somebody else. Poor man, you are the last one in the line, so they thought that you would be punished. On the contrary, I am so satisfied that I am giving you one thousand rupees."

Then the king fined each and every one of the worker's superiors one thousand rupees, right from his minister on down, because each one said that he was too busy and somebody else should do it. The minister, his assistant and his assistant's assistant, everybody, was fined. After the king collected all the fines, he presented the entire amount to the poor worker.

The king said to him, "If I had said that I was very, very pleased with the pond, the minister would have been the first one to say, 'I did it. I did it.' He would have claimed all the credit. But my minister is such a rogue. He went to somebody else, and then that person went to somebody else, and so on. I wanted to know who had actually dug the pond so that I could reward that person. I am so happy to have an excellent worker like you."

A spiritual aspirant can be sincere to his friends, relatives, neighbours and to the world at large, but he may not be sincere to himself. It is infinitely easier to be sincere to others than to oneself. In his day-to-day life in the outside world, an aspirant almost always speaks the truth, but unfortunately constantly tells lies to himself. It is his ardent promise to himself that he will not doubt himself, he will not fear anything, he will not be a victim to impurity and anxiety. Every day he makes an inner promise to his soul, to God, that he will be divine, he will be a chosen instrument of God, he will listen only to the dictates of his inner being. But the moment he comes out of his room and enters into the wide world, all his promises are broken as the day advances. His outer promises he very often keeps, but the inner promise to himself he cannot keep. Yet the inner promise has to be fulfilled first and foremost.

If you are not sincere,
God will ask others
To investigate your authenticity.
If you are sincere,
God will allow you
Not only to investigate Him,
But also to take anything you want or need
From Him.

Truth And Falsehood

Spirituality needs and demands sincerity from beginning to end. If we have no sincerity, then it is useless for us to enter into the spiritual life. In ordinary life, we may be insincere and still become successful. But in our spiritual life we do not get even an iota of success if we are not sincere. Only a sincere seeker can make true spiritual progress.

Just as we develop muscles, we can also develop our sincerity. But what we need is a constant inner urge. Otherwise, one moment we will be sincere and the next moment we will be insincere. Our life will be like day and night, like light and darkness. But if our inner aspiration is constant and spontaneous, then the very urge, the very flow of our aspiration, will compel us to be sincere.

If we take falsehood as our very own, what happens? Truth remains silent. But if we are eager to follow the truth, then falsehood comes and strikes us, insults us, discourages us. At the same time, truth is not extremely eager to have us as its very own because it has seen how many times we have touched its feet and promised that we would listen to it, but time and again this has been all false promises and idle talk. We say that we will follow the path of truth, but the next moment we go and listen to falsehood because we get more pleasure there.

40

When we really do try to fulfil the promise that we made to truth, we may feel falsehood pulling at our mind. "Where are you going?" it says. "You promised me that you would always remain with me." But if the day comes when truth sees that we are absolutely sincere, at that time it fights most powerfully against falsehood. And if we become totally one with truth, we will see that all the dark forces inside us and around us have no choice but to surrender. A supreme test is going on between purity and impurity in our nature. When truth is convinced that our promise is absolutely sincere, that even if we do not get the inner light immediately, we will not go back to falsehood, that our choice is light and nothing else, it will dispossess falsehood totally.

Be brave
Where your heart is concerned.
Be sincere
Where your mind is concerned.
Then you will see how easy it is
To live your life
In a supremely better consciousness.

Sincerity Speeds Your Spiritual Progress

In order to enter any spiritual path, a seeker must start with an inner cry. If a child cries on the first floor and the mother happens to be on the third floor, the mother comes down to the child because she knows that the cry of the child is intense, sincere and genuine. A child is not taught by the mother how to cry. She does not say, "If you cry, then I will give you milk." No, it comes spontaneously. When he needs some milk, he cries. Similarly, when our inner cry is sincere and genuine, God feeds us with His Compassion-Light.

41

At every moment the Inner Pilot will guide you if you follow a specific path most sincerely and devotedly. You can easily know whether you are ready for a spiritual path or not. When you are hungry, you know that you need to eat something. In the inner life also, when you are hungry for peace, light and bliss, at that time you are ready. When you have that inner cry, that inner need for something, then you are ready for a spiritual path.

Sincerity travels along the straight path, the sunlit path, the short path, whereas the path of insincerity is dark and full of thorns. Sincerity is necessary, along with readiness. If you are ready and also sincere, then naturally you will go very far.

It finally dawned on me
That I could also try to become
A choice instrument
Of my Lord Supreme.

Finding Your Path

A spiritual Teacher is like a boat. If you are in one boat, you are safe. But if you keep one leg in one boat and the other leg in another boat, then you will just fall into the sea of ignorance. If you are securely seated in a boat, then the boatman is capable of taking you to the other shore. Then, once you reach your destination, you will see that all the boats arrived by different routes. The goal is one, but the paths are many. You cannot constantly change paths and hope to make the same speed.

In the spiritual life, there are some teachers who can instruct you for a couple of years and there are those who can teach you right from the kindergarten level to the highest university courses. Even if a teacher is sincere, if he does not have the capacity to take you to the highest, naturally you will leave him when you have gone as far as he can take you. Again, there are so-called Masters who do not have the capacity to teach at all, but who will try to keep you just to exploit you. Your inner being will tell you whether you are making satisfactory progress or not. There is a saying, "When the student is ready, the teacher appears." If the aspirant is sincerely crying for a path, he will definitely find one.

The Officer Finds His Master

Once a well-known military officer decided to accept the spiritual life. He wanted to give up the world of attachment for good, so he began praying to God every day to take him to his real Guru. One night in a dream he saw a most beautiful luminous being, and at the same time he saw a word written on his heart: "Nigamananda." This officer knew nothing about Swami Nigamananda, who was then living a thousand miles away in a different city. But the officer made inquiries, and soon he found someone who knew of Nigamananda and could tell him where the Master was to be found.

In a few days' time the officer-seeker reached Nigamananda's ashram. As soon as he reached Nigamananda, he knew that this was the Master he had seen in his dream and fell at his feet.

Nigamananda said to him simply, "So you believe in dreams?"

To look
Into your Master's eye
Is to enter
Into your own unexplored universe.

43

Your Private Tutor

I have been asked many times whether having a spiritual Master or Guru is necessary for God-realisation. A living Guru is not absolutely indispensable. The first person on earth who realised God, had no human Guru. But if you have a Guru, it facilitates your inner spiritual progress. Why go to university when you can study at home? Because you feel that you will get expert instruction from people who know the subject well. Now, you know that there have been a few – very, very few – individuals of real knowledge who did not go to any university. Every rule has its exceptions. God is in everybody, and if a seeker feels that he does not need human help, he is most welcome to try his capacity alone. But if someone is wise and wants to run towards his Goal, instead of stumbling or merely walking, then certainly the help of a Guru can be considerable.

As we need teachers to help us acquire outer knowledge, so also we need a spiritual Master to help and guide us in our inner life, especially in the beginning. Otherwise, our progress will be very slow and uncertain, and we may become terribly confused. We will get high, elevating experiences, but we will not give them adequate significance. Doubt may eclipse our mind and we will say, "I am just an ordinary person, so how can I have this kind of experience? Perhaps I am deluding myself." Or we will tell our friends, and they will say, "It is all mental hallucination. Forget about the spiritual life." But if there is a spiritual Master who knows what the Reality is, the Master will encourage and inspire the seeker and give him the proper explanations of his experiences. Again, if the seeker is doing something wrong in his meditation, the Master will be in a position to correct him.

A Guru is your private tutor in the spiritual life. There is a big difference between a private tutor and an ordinary teacher. An ordinary teacher will look at a student's paper and then give him a mark. He will examine the student and then pass him or fail him. But the private tutor is not like that. He encourages and inspires the student at home so that he can pass his examination.

A God-knower-Master
Helps me to stand
On Eternity's Shore,
Helps me to open
Immortality's Door
And
Helps me to enter
Infinity's Core.

How To Recognise A Genuine Master

A real spiritual Master is one who has attained God-realisation. Everyone is one with God, but the real spiritual Master has established his conscious oneness with God. At any moment he can enter into a higher consciousness and bring down messages from God to those disciples who have faith in him. The Master, if he is genuine, represents God on earth for those seekers who have real aspiration and faith in him. He has been authorised or commissioned by God to help them. The real Teacher, the real Guru, is God Himself. But on earth He will often operate in and through a spiritual Master. The Master energises the seeker with inspiration and, in the course of time, through the infinite Grace of the Supreme, offers the seeker illumination.

How can an aspirant know if a Master professing to be realised is actually realised? A God-realised spiritual Master is not someone with wings and a halo to identify him. He is normal, except that in his inner life he has abundant peace, light and bliss. If you come to a spiritual Master expecting something other than this, you will be disappointed. But again, you must know if you are fit to judge. In the spiritual life, a real seeker who has sincere aspiration and dedication has already achieved a little bit of inner light, and with that light he is bound to see and feel something in a true spiritual Master. An unrealised Master can fool you for a day or a month or a few years, but he cannot fool you forever. Your sincerity is your safeguard. Even if a Master is genuine, he may not be meant for you. How do you know when you have found your own Master? It is like this. There may be many people around you, but when you see a particular person, immediately you experience some joy. In that case you have to know that this person has some inner connection with you. And if you have an inner connection with a genuine Master, the moment you see that particular Master, you will be given joy. The spiritual Master who gives you immediate joy, spontaneous joy, boundless joy, is your Master.

Sometimes, if you are lucky enough, you may find your own Master the first time you see one. On the other hand, you may have to go to quite a few spiritual Masters. But there is no seeker on earth who will remain without a Teacher if he is desperately in need of one. If his aspiration is intense, if his inner cry is constantly mounting, how can God remain asleep? It is God who has kindled the flame of aspiration in that particular seeker, and it is God who will bring a spiritual Master to him or place him at the feet of a Master.

The Guru carries
The heavy load of suffering
From this shore
And brings back the Smile
From the other shore.

Listening To The Inner Pilot

There are various ways to increase one's inner drive, inner urge. If you are an absolute beginner and eager to enter into the spiritual life, then the first thing to do is pray to God. Prayer should be very simple, very sincere and spontaneous. Prayer is most effective in the early stages of the spiritual life, and it is prayer that will increase the inner urge in a truth-seeker.

At the beginning, when someone is just curious or a little bit sincere, we cannot call that person a real seeker. If he is a step ahead in the spiritual realm, he will not be satisfied with the rest of the world or even with himself. He wants a better creation in himself, and in the world at large. Then he has to feel the necessity of the fulfilment of God's Will on earth and of taking a conscious part in fulfilling God's creation. Such being the case, God is bound to give him an additional amount of inner urge. Then, if a time comes when the aspirant feels that he needs only God, he becomes the real pride and real instrument of God. At that time, automatically, his aspiration is increased in boundless measure from deep within.

Again, if you want to increase your inner drive, in general you can do it just by accepting the life of sincerity and the life of dedication. If you have a Master, then you have to be absolutely sincere to the Master. But if you do not have a Master, what should you do? You have to go deep within and try to feel the Inner Pilot. The Inner Pilot will speak through your conscience. You may not see the Inner Pilot – to see Him, the Supreme, is a very rare experience – but the Inner Pilot is always ready to act through your conscience. And if you listen to the dictates of your conscience, then naturally your aspiration is bound to increase.

My Eternity's Beloved Pilot Supreme,
I know, I know,
I came into the world
For only one purpose:
To give You the utmost joy
In Your own Way.

One-Pointed Pursuit Of The Goal

While you are following the spiritual life, if you are attacked by undivine forces or if you feel that your aspiration is not as it should be, never give up your spiritual life. Every day you cannot eat the most delicious food, but still you eat every day in order to keep your body fit so you can go to work, go to school and do normal activities. In the spiritual life, when we meditate, what do we actually do? We feed the soul, our inner being. Now, if we cannot feed the soul most delightfully every day, we must not give up trying. It is better to feed the soul something than to allow it to starve. Never give up; always try to meditate.

Meditation does not mean just sitting quietly for five or ten minutes. It requires conscious effort. The mind has to be made calm and quiet; at the same time, it has to be vigilant so as not to allow any distracting thoughts or desires to enter. When you can make the mind calm and quiet, your whole existence becomes an empty vessel, and your inner being can invoke infinite peace, light and bliss to enter into the vessel and fill it. This is meditation.

The road to God-realisation is long. Sometimes while walking along the road you will see beautiful trees with flowers, foliage and fruits. Psychic powers may come on the way to realisation, but they are like delicious fruits on the way to the Goal. If somebody walks along a road and finds them, then he may be tempted to stop his journey. He will acquire psychic powers and then not want to pray or meditate any more. Instead, he will want to use his powers to try to read somebody's mind. Acquiring occult power has taken many, many sincere seekers away from the Truth.

Sincerity means that you want only the goal, and not the flowers and fruits that are along the road. Sometimes you will see that there is only a road, and there are no trees on either side. Sometimes you may feel that you are on an endless road through a barren desert, and that the goal is still impossibly far away. But do not give up walking just because the distance seems far. In order to realise God you have to go forward untiringly. Even spiritual Masters have gone through dry periods in their inner life. So for beginners in the spiritual life to have this kind of experience is not at all blameworthy. Take dryness as darkness. Think of going through a tunnel. You know that there will be some light at the end because you have been through tunnels before. After you enter, for some time you know that there may be no light, but if you have patience, you know that you will see light.

No more teeming problems
Will be able to crowd
Along my life's path,
For I can clearly see
That a new age of love and promise
Is dawning within me.

The Patience Of A Farmer

Some people cry for light sincerely but without satisfactory results, simply because God's destined Hour has not yet arrived. If a farmer feels that on the day he starts working hard to cultivate his land he should get a bumper crop, he will be disgusted and abandon the field when he sees no result after a few weeks of sincere effort. But although sincerity is important, time is still a great factor. The field can only produce satisfactory fruit in God's own time. Our timing and God's timing need not be, and very often are not, the same. The seeker of the infinite Truth must have the patience of a farmer.

To have a sincere longing does not mean that one cannot have patience. A kindergarten student sees that his brother has got a Master's degree. He has a sincere longing for a Master's degree as well, but he knows that it will take him twenty years to get it. If he does not pay attention to his studies now, then he will not pass his examination. Then how will he go on to high school and university? Right now he is the seed. Gradually the seed will germinate and become a tiny plant. Finally it will become a huge banyan tree. Does the seed think that by some miracle it will turn into a banyan tree overnight? No, it is absurd. There has to be an evolutionary process of gradual development.

If you feel that each moment is leading you towards your destination, then this progress itself is a kind of partial goal. You cannot separate divine progress, real progress, from your goal. Rather than fighting against time, you should try your utmost to derive spiritual benefit, spiritual progress, from each second. Each time you make progress, you have to feel that you have touched something of the goal itself, a tiny portion. In this way, you will feel that you are really advancing.

At this very moment, in the twinkling of an eye, you want to realise God. This is your own sense of need. But if you feel that God needs your realisation infinitely more than you need it, then you see that it becomes His responsibility. God takes this responsibility on His shoulders most sincerely. After all, it is He who wants to manifest in and through us. And if we remain unrealised, then how can He fulfil Himself in and through us? But we have to know that He has His own choice time. On our part we have only to be earnest, sincere, dedicated, devoted and surrendered to His Will.

Everything that we want to accomplish, we have to do on the strength of our sincerity. If we are seekers, we have to pray and meditate. If we are sincere and patient at every moment, then we will have real satisfaction in our achievement. Our present satisfaction may not be the ultimate satisfaction, but we can rest assured that the ultimate satisfaction is bound to grow and evolve in us. Satisfaction comes when we feel that we are making constant progress, going higher or deeper. First we feel that we are progressing towards something unknowable, then towards something knowable. Finally we realise not only that the Goal was always ours, but also that it is what we have always, eternally been.

> *Your surrender-acceptance*
> *Of God's Will*
> *Has created a new hope*
> *For the entire world.*

Purity

Your purity has the capacity
To unlock everybody's heart-door.
Something more:
Your purity is the only reality-passport
Which enables you to enter into
Each and every human heart.

Purity is the light of the soul expressing its divinity through the body, the vital and the mind. When we are pure, we gain everything. Today we may have great thoughts or great inner power, but tomorrow we are bound to lose them if we are not pure. But if we can retain our purity, we will never lose anything worth keeping.

All spiritual aspirants, without exception, have seen and felt the necessity of purity. If there is no purity in the aspirant's inner or outer life, he cannot retain any of the spiritual gifts he receives. Everything will disappear and everything will disappoint the seeker if he is wanting in purity. But if he is flooded with purity, the divine qualities will all eventually enter into him.

Purity is actually the vessel inside us that holds light, peace, bliss and power. These and other divine qualities can never stay in us permanently if we are wanting in purity. Some people have many spiritual experiences, but they lose them immediately. Why? Because they do not have enough purity, in spite of the inner depth and height of their experiences. And thousands fall from the spiritual life entirely just because they do not bother to establish purity in their lives. They aspire for two months, three months, six months, five years, ten years.

Then all of a sudden they fall, just because they do not have purity. Today they climb the inner Mount Everest, but tomorrow they fall down into the lowest abyss. Purity lost, everything is lost; God Himself is lost. But purity won, the world is won; the entire universe is won.

If you can keep
Pure thoughts in your mind
During the day,
Then at night you will be blessed
With the company of angels.

The Power Of Purity

We should try to feel what purity actually is. Purity is not something weak or negative; it is something soulful and dynamic. If we feel that purity is something liquid, like water, or something weak, elastic or delicate, like a toy, then purity will not increase at all in our being. But if we feel that purity is something very powerful, it can create a new life inside us and around us. Purity is fed constantly by the infinite Energy and the indomitable, adamantine Will of the Supreme.

Once purity is established, especially in the vital, much is accomplished in one's inner life and outer life. If we have the feeling that purity is something that will give us a new life, a new world of peace, bliss and dynamic power, then our purity will immediately increase. When we are aware that purity can do much for us, we will value it properly.

In purity there is divine magic. If we can hold one single pure thought during our meditation, then for hours we will derive benefit from that pure thought. During that time our worst weaknesses are transformed into real strengths. We all know that quantity and quality are not the same. We all care for quality and not for quantity. But with purity, quality and quantity go together. Purity is like a divine magnet. It pulls all divine qualities into us. The more we develop divine purity, the greater becomes our inner strength.

I am not
A weeping weakling.
I am
God's own Confidence-Strength
In the depths of my heart.

One Step At A Time

A seeker cannot achieve inner purification all at once. It is a gradual process. For a month we may be absolutely pure in our mind, in our vital and in our physical, but if there is no permanence, after a while this purity will be totally lost. But once we have a little purity, then we are inspired, energised. If we get purity for five minutes, then we know that purity exists. We see that we have got something real, although it may not last. Even the purity which is transient will give us joy. Then we will try to get more joy by achieving something permanent.

If we want purity permanently, we have to enter wholeheartedly into the life of aspiration. If we want to have something lasting, we have to meditate on the soul, not to purify the soul, but to spread the light of the soul to all parts of our being. When we meditate on the soul, we have to pray to the Inner Pilot or to our soul to give us lasting purity in the heart. We bring the soul's purity into the heart and from there it enters into the mind. After that it enters into the vital and then into the body.

Inner purification begins with our conscious meditation, then it has to be achieved during our waking hours, then during our sleep. After all these it can be done in the dream state. We have to start at the beginning and work in sequence. In order to invoke purity during your meditation, whenever you meditate at home, try to burn incense and candles and have flowers and the picture of your Guru, if you have one. These things will help to establish purity in the atmosphere. Then when you begin your meditation, try to breathe in and out for three to five minutes while imagining that you are breathing in and out with your Master or the highest within you. Then you can enter into your meditation with tremendous purity.

Now for the waking hours. If you cannot purify your daily actions, then how are you going to make progress? Again, if you make progress, then only can you purify your life. These things go together. If you meditate well, then only can you think of loving and serving God. Again, if you serve God devotedly and unconditionally, then only can you think of meditating well. As action and meditation go together, so purity in your day-to-day life and spiritual progress must go together; they are complementary. You should have purity in your thoughts, in your ideas, in your feelings, in your conversation, in all that you say, all that you do, all that you feel and all that you are.

If you think of purity, impurity cannot come. If you look only at light, light, light, then where is the darkness? If you think of purity, then impurity goes away. So only stay in purity; just remain in the room that is all illumined. Always do the positive thing. When impurity knocks at your heart's door, do not allow it to enter.

The Inner Shrine

Purity is like a muscle that can be built up through exercise and practise. It is not an easy thing to achieve. You need many years of practise and also God's Grace. But if you try to achieve purity, certainly you will get it.

The soul always remains pure, no matter what goes on around it. But purity has to be established in the physical, in the vital, in the mind and in the heart. You are crying for purity in the heart. You may get it in a few days or a few months, let us say. But it takes more time to get purity in the mind. In the vital it is still more difficult. In the physical, God alone knows how many years it takes.

Human beings have purity to some extent in the heart. If you do not have purity in abundant measure, if countless earthly desires are in possession of your heart, then before concentrating on the heart, you should invoke purity. Purity is the feeling of having a living shrine deep in the inmost recesses of your heart. When you feel the divine presence of an inner shrine, automatically you are purified.

O Lord Supreme,
Give me a pure heart
So that my purity-heart
Can always feel
Not only who You are to me,
But also who I am to You.

Purity In The Mind

In the mind the quantity of purity is very small. The mind is always subject to doubt, fear, worry and anxiety. It is always assailed by wrong thoughts and wrong movements. As soon as a thought enters our mind, we have to see whether or not it is a pure thought. A pure thought is a thought that expands itself and our consciousness. The mind can be purified by cherishing only those thoughts that expand.

You can think of the mind as a vessel. The vessel is full of dirty, filthy water, let us say. If you empty it, only then do you get the opportunity to fill it up again with pure water. If the mind is empty, that means already you have made considerable progress. You have emptied out ignorance, worry, imperfection, limitation and all undivine things. Now what will you do? You will fill this empty vessel with joy, love, purity and all divine qualities. Or, you can think of the mind as a dark room that has not seen light for many, many years. You need someone who can bring light into this room. That person is the soul. You have to invoke this most intimate friend who has the capacity to help you and the willingness to illumine anything that is dark within you. You have to consciously feel that you need the soul just as you need the body. If your need is sincere and genuine, then the soul will come forward and illumine the darkness that you have in your mind. The moment the mind is surcharged with divine light, it is illumined. This mind is conscious of the soul's capacity, the soul's reality and the soul's mission, and it will gladly help the soul.

Each soulful thought
In my mind
Adds to the beauty and purity
Of my heart's glistening chandelier.

Purity In The Vital

In the vital, purity is mixed with impurity. There dynamism and aggression play together, but aggression is impurity and dynamism is purity. At the present stage of evolution, most human beings live in the undivine vital, where all is desire, anxiety and excitement.

Selfish demands are made by the vital. If the vital demands something, we want to get it by hook or by crook. Usually a vital demand is a desire that comes from a very low plane of consciousness. It tempts us to lead a very undivine and corrupted life. Further, a vital demand is always destructive. It does not embody any light and, at the same time, it does not care for light.

God gave us the dynamic, energetic, all-conquering vital to use for a divine purpose. But God also gave us limited freedom, and we have not used this freedom properly. God is like the father who gives his child a penny because he wants to see what the child will do with it. If the child uses it properly, then the father gives him a nickel, a dime, a quarter.

When God gave us the vital, He wanted us to expand it. He wanted us to spread the wings of dynamic energy so that we could put an end to the life of ignorance. Think of your vital as a bird, and try to imagine you are unfolding and spreading your wings. While you are expanding and spreading your wings, your vital is becoming dynamic. This way you can easily offer your soul's perfection to your vital.

Human Love Versus Divine Love

Very often people do not know the difference between the heart and the vital, because the vital is near the heart. There are three principal channels through which our life-energy flows. These meet together at different places, and each meeting place forms a centre. Indian spiritual philosophy calls these centres *chakras*. The spiritual heart, or *anahata chakra*, is in the centre of the chest, and the vital is at the navel and below. From the navel, the consciousness flows upward, and people think it is the consciousness of the heart. Then the emotionally and physically impure vital consciousness flows outward, and people think that it is the heart's consciousness purifying and illumining the whole world.

Unless one aspires, it is very difficult to know the difference between human love and the heart's divine love. The vital emotion always creates attachment, but people are convinced that this is their heart's concern. Why is human love attachment? Because it constantly demands and is conditional.

Human love and divine love are two completely different things. If I give you fifteen cents and you give me a piece of candy, that is called human love. But in divine love, you do not wait for my fifteen cents. You give me the piece of candy cheerfully of your own accord. In human love, we display the buyer's and seller's love which is synonymous with self-interest. Ordinary human love is always full of expectation. With our human love we feel, "I have done so much for that person; certainly he will also do something for me." I am not saying that human beings cannot express divine love. They can and sometimes do. But consistent divine love is, at present, rare in human beings.

You can easily tell whether your love is vital or pure, whether it is human love or divine love. When your love is vital, there is a conscious demand or at least an unconscious expectation from the love you offer to others. When your love is pure or spiritual, there is no demand, no expectation. There is only the sweetest feeling of spontaneous oneness, like a mother who gives and gives and gives to her child simply because she loves him.

It is not only possible, but absolutely necessary, to prevent ourselves from giving impure vital love. We have to use love not to bind or possess the world, but to free and widen our own consciousness and the consciousness of the world. What we must do is to bring the heart's purifying and transforming love into the impure vital. The vital, as such, is not bad at all. When it is controlled, purified and transformed, it becomes a most significant instrument of God.

What has soulful purity
Done for me?
It has richly helped me
To spread my oneness-love
Here, there and all-where.
Try to achieve it.
You will succeed.

59

Go Slowly, Steadily

We have to know how seriously we take the spiritual life. Millions of people are still asleep and are not consciously aspiring for God-realisation. They can do whatever they want with their lives. Those who have just awakened should try to purify their lives slowly.

If you tell a beginner that he has to give up all his lower vital propensities the moment he enters into the spiritual life, he will never enter into the spiritual life at all. If you enter into the spiritual life and say, "Today I am going to conquer all my lower vital propensities," then tomorrow your mind will doubt the necessity of this self-denial and your vital will torture you in every way. If it is not ready, it will revolt under this harsh discipline and destroy your aspiration, or your body will resist and break down. Go slowly, steadily. As you make progress in the spiritual life, automatically the necessity for lower vital activity diminishes. Those who are really advanced find that the life of pleasure is replaced by the life of real joy.

Start to think of a new life.
Your sincere mind
Will teach you how to start.
Your pure heart
Will continue for you.
Just start to think of a new life.

Purity In The Physical

How can you aspire for purity in the physical? It is through constant elevating prayer and constant inner cry for light. Pray for and meditate on the inner light, the higher light, so that light can enter into your system and illumine you. Purity in the physical can be established only by bringing down light from Above into the physical. Inner purity also depends to some extent on outer cleanliness. Some spiritual people neglect physical cleanliness. They do not feel that it is important. But we care for the physical because it is in the physical that the soul lives, and because the fulfilment of the divine mission can only take place on earth in and through the physical body. Therefore, we have to keep the body pure. When we have established purity in all parts of our nature, only then can the divine power last permanently in us. We should try to have cleanliness, which is outer purity. We should shower or bathe daily, and while doing this, we should feel consciously not only that we are getting cleanliness but also that actual purification of the outer body is taking place.

Aspiration And The Vegetarian Diet

Many spiritual seekers have come to the conclusion that a vegetarian is in a position to make quick progress in the spiritual life. If we eat meat, the aggressive animal consciousness enters into us. Our nerves become agitated and restless, and this can interfere with our meditation. If a seeker does not stop eating meat, generally he does not get subtle experiences, subtle visions or subtle realisations.

Some people feel that it is meat that gives them strength. But when they go deep within, they discover that it is their own idea about meat that is giving them strength. One can change that idea and feel that it is not meat but the spiritual energy pervading one's body that gives one strength. That energy comes from meditation as well as from proper nourishment. The strength that one can get from aspiration and meditation is infinitely more than the strength one gets from eating meat.

The mild qualities of fruits and vegetables help us to establish the qualities of sweetness, softness, simplicity and purity in our inner life as well as in our outer life. If we are vegetarians, it helps our inner being to strengthen its own existence. Inwardly we are praying and meditating; outwardly the food we are taking from Mother Earth is helping us too, giving us not only energy but aspiration.

Along with a vegetarian diet, we must pray and meditate. If we have aspiration, the vegetarian diet will help considerably; the body's purity will help our inner aspiration to become more intense and more soulful. But the real purity comes from the inner aspiration of the soul. Those who give all importance to food in order to achieve purity in the mind, heart and soul are making a mistake. If we really want purity, it is good not to eat meat, but we have to know that it is aspiration and meditation that are of paramount importance. When we combine our inner purity with our outer purity, we strengthen them both. But inner purity must be given first importance.

Vigilance, Not Arrogance

The present-day world is full of impurity. It seems that purity is a currency from another world. If you feel there is much impurity where you work, if your colleagues are full of impurity, then you have to be more careful, more conscious. You have to concentrate more on purity in your life. At every moment you have to feel that there is a struggle going on between your aspiration and the pull of the material world.

But if you have the feeling that you are far more spiritual or more pure than others around you, then it will be all self-deception. You may think that you have more spirituality, more purity, but who knows? Someone else may have more spirituality and humility and other divine qualities. Unfortunately, many people who enter the spiritual life look down on others, thinking, "They do not go to any spiritual centre, they do not go to church, they do not pray, they do not have purity." This is a false aggrandisement of the ego.

There was once a very great spiritual Master whose name was Troilanga Swami. He was the possessor of tremendous occult and spiritual power. One day he was with his disciples when a nicely-dressed middle-aged Bengali gentleman wearing a new dhoti and perfumed with oil came to him. To the disciples' surprise, Troilanga Swami embraced the gentleman.

Everybody said, "How can you embrace someone who is so sophisticated and unspiritual? There is no spirituality in him."

Troilanga Swami said to them, "You fools, you do not recognise him. You people would have to give up everything in life, renounce everything, in order to come to his spiritual state of consciousness. In your highest state of consciousness you cannot equal him. For him to wear clean, new, ironed clothes, or to use perfume, is nothing. He has reached such a spiritual height that he will not be affected no matter what he does. You cannot judge people by their outer appearance. He is a really great seeker, an extraordinary soul." Troilanga Swami's words proved true. The man's name was Shyama Charan Lahiri and he was later known to be a great spiritual Master.

If we are really pure, then we do not see impurity in others. Even a person who is living in the world can have a childlike attitude. To be childlike does not mean to be childish. We can be simple, sincere and spontaneous in our dealings with the sophisticated world without being stupid or foolish. We can have implicit faith in God's protection and guidance even while living and working in the ordinary world.

Real spiritual people are not at all disturbed by impurity, because they have tremendous inner light and that light saves them. Let us face the world. Let us take life as it comes. Then the undercurrents of our inner, spiritual life will always flow on unnoticed, unobstructed, unafraid.

When you are right,
Everything around you is right,
Because the beautiful flow
That is inside your heart
Has the capacity to spread its fragrance
Of oneness-light
Around you.

Exercises To Try

The very utterance of the word "purity" can help to change your outer life as well as your inner life. Repeat the word "purity" one hundred and eight times daily, placing your right hand on your navel as you say it. Then you will see that abundant purity will enter into you and flow through you.

You can also look at your Master's picture or you can look at yourself in the mirror. If you concentrate on your own reflection, feel that you are totally one with the physical being that you are seeing. Then try to enter into the image that you are seeing. From there you should try to grow with one thought: "God wants me, and I need God." Then you will see that slowly, steadily and gradually this divine thought is entering into you and permeating your inner and outer existence, giving you purity in your mind, vital and body.

Another effective way to attain purity is through conscious offering of your life-breath to the Supreme. Early in the morning breathe in consciously seven times, and while you breathe in, try to feel that you are actually breathing in through your heart and not through your nose. Try to feel that your breath is entering you through your heart centre. And while you are breathing out, try to feel that your breath is going up, up to the top of your head and out through the "thousand-petalled lotus", the crown centre at the top of your head.

If you can feel, and not just imagine, that you are breathing through your heart, immediately purity will enter and start revolving and functioning in you.

When you breathe in, you have to feel that you are breathing in nothing but purity. It is not your mental imagination; it is the actual feeling that the air you are breathing is nothing but purity. When purity enters, it is like a current going from the soles of the feet to the crown of the head. Everything inside is being purified by this current.

When purity starts performing its role, impurity from the navel and lower centres travels up and is released into something which is beyond the mind. Do this early in the morning and in the evening also, if possible. Then your system is bound to be purified.

I purify my body
By chanting God's Name.
I purify my vital
By serving God.
I purify my mind
By emptying my mind for God.
I purify my heart
By meditating on God's Compassion-Love.

The Fragrance Of A Flower

If you can establish some purity on the strength of your very best meditation, then the best way to preserve it is to feel that you have a most fragrant rose inside your heart. From time to time, try to feel its presence, smell its fragrance and see its beauty. If you have a flower right in front of you, sometimes with your eye you appreciate the beauty, sometimes inwardly with your heart you feel your oneness with its beauty. If you can see, smell and feel a flower in your heart, then you are bound to feel throughout the day the purity that you achieved during your best meditation early in the morning.

Also, during the day you can offer your breath to God consciously at least twenty times. In this way you can become pure in all aspects of your being. When you consciously offer your life-breath, it should be with your purest love and dedication. As you breathe in, you should feel that the purity of the whole universe is entering into you and purifying your entire existence. When you breathe in consciously, you should try to feel purity in the mind, purity in the vital and purity in the physical.

When you have offered your life-breath, you are as pure as a flower. The very nature of a flower is to spread fragrance. The flower may not talk to you and tell you, "Look, I have purity! I am now giving it to you, so take it, take it!" But the very fact that you are near a flower will immediately bring you purity. Similarly, when you yourself have purity, automatically it will flow.

Purity is the conscious feeling of oneness with the Highest. Purity is something we must have inside us all the time, not something we can get from somewhere else when we need it. Purity is something to be lived.

We must feel that the world is not around us or in front of us, but deep within us; therefore, we have to try to achieve our own purification and the transformation of our nature. The more we are inwardly purified and transformed, the sooner the world's transformation will take place. When we have purity, the world is filled with pride in us. If Mother Earth houses a single pure soul, her joy knows no bounds. She says, "Here, at least, is a soul I can rely upon."

Each pure thought
Is indeed
Blessing-light
From Heaven.

Aspiration

Be brave!
You will see that your heart's
Soaring aspiration-flames
Cannot be bound by anything.

Aspiration is a glowing flame that secretly and sacredly uplifts our consciousness and finally liberates us. Unlike other flames, this flame does not burn anything. It purifies, illumines and transforms our life. Aspiration is our inner urge to transcend both the experience and the realisation already achieved. Aspiration is an inner hunger for God's Love, Light and Bliss. It is aspiration that can take us to the highest, to the deepest, to the farthest. Aspiration can create miracles in us at every second.

Aspiration is a cry within our heart. This cry is not for name and fame. This cry is for our total, unconditional, unreserved oneness with the Inner Pilot. Aspiration is the soul's mounting cry to reach the Highest and to bring down the Highest into the earth's consciousness. If we can remain in the heart, we will begin to feel this inner cry, and we can enter into the divine consciousness through it.

If anybody wants to know whether his aspiration is genuine and whether he is really marching towards the Goal or not, then I wish to ask that person to observe his mind and heart. If in his mind he feels inner joy and peace, and if his heart is flooded with joy and delight, not pleasure, then his aspiration is true and genuine.

Inspiration, Aspiration And Inner Joy

In the spiritual life we use the term "inner awakening". Awakening is the beginning of the soul's journey towards the ultimate Goal. At every moment the inner awakening has to be fed and nurtured by our constant aspiration. If we want to achieve anything whatsoever, inspiration is necessary. In the spiritual life this inspiration we can get by reading sacred books written by genuine spiritual Masters. But when inspiration has played its role, we have to enter into the world of aspiration. We have to try to live the wisdom of the books.

Not fear, not wory, not doubt,
But aspiration-flames
Will today adorn
The shrine of my heart.

The Highest Goal

If someone is awakened, then naturally that person will run towards his Goal. But the spiritual life is voluntary; it is a matter of personal choice. When you are ready, when your hour has struck, you will get up and run towards your Goal. Then, after a while, somebody else will be ready and he will run towards his Goal. The spiritual life is not like a race, where everyone starts at the same time and from the same starting point. When you are ready, you will have your starting point; when I am ready, I will have mine. But the Goal is always the same. You may start your journey a few hours or a few years ahead of me, but when you reach your destination and I reach my destination, it will be the same place.

But this is true only if it is the ultimate, the highest Goal. Otherwise, your goal may be just to have an iota of peace, light and bliss. When you come to that place, you are satisfied and you do not want

68

to have anything more. On your way to the ultimate destination you will reach some partial goal and perhaps think that this is the final Goal. Then you will stay there for some time. But when I reach that goal, I may want to go further. Then naturally I will cover more distance. But when I reach my ultimate Goal and when you reach your ultimate Goal, it will be the same, for everyone's ultimate Goal is the same. There is only one Goal for each human being and that Goal is God-realisation.

Again, we have to know that there is no end to our realisation, there is no end to our God-manifestation, there is no end to our perfection. Perfect perfection is not a stationary goal. No. There is no end to our journey, because God is not and cannot be satisfied with any particular standard. God Himself is always transcending His own Reality. We, who are His conscious, chosen instruments, are also doing the same.

> *A realisation-soul*
> *Is a freedom-bird*
> *That flies*
> *In God's Bliss-dancing Sky.*

Two Tragedies

In the apt words of George Bernard Shaw, "There are two tragedies in life. One is not to get your heart's desire; the other is to get it." If we remain in the world of desire, we will never be able to fulfil ourselves. As a child, we have millions of desires, and even when we reach the age of seventy, we see that a particular desire has not been fulfilled and we feel miserable. We want one house, then two houses; one car, then two cars. There is no limit to it.

Some people are under the impression that desire and aspiration are the same thing. Unfortunately – or, rather, fortunately – that is not true. The difference between the two is very simple and clear. Desire wants to bind and devour the world. Aspiration wishes to free and feed the world. Desire is the outgoing energy. Aspiration is the inflowing light.

Needless to say, it is our aspiration, our mounting inner cry, that leads us to the Kingdom of Heaven: a plane full of peace and delight. We feel it when we reside deep within ourselves and when we transcend our egocentric individual consciousness. The higher we go beyond our limited consciousness, the quicker we enter into our deepest, infinite consciousness, and the more intimately we shall see, feel and possess the Kingdom of Heaven within ourselves.

Desire is expectation. No expectation, no frustration. Desire killed, true happiness built. Desire is temptation. Temptation nourished, true happiness starved. Aspiration is awakening. The soul's awakening is the birth of supernal delight.

My desire to know,
My desire to love
And my desire to become
Divine and perfect
Are my only desires in life.

The King And The Sword

A great Indian king once went on a boat trip on the Ganges River. He and his attendants saw a man swimming behind them. It was Troilanga Swami. It happened, in an hour or so, that Troilanga Swami swam near the boat smiling, so they helped him into it. The people all knew him and had tremendous respect, love and veneration for him. The king too was pleased to see him, because he also admired him.

The king had a sword hanging around his waist. Troilanga Swami took it from him and examined it and played with it like a child. Then he suddenly threw it into the Ganges. The king was furious. He had received this sword for his valour and merit, so he felt miserable that he had lost such a precious thing. He wanted to punish Troilanga Swami, but everybody protested: "Oh no, he is a saint; you cannot do that. It will be a terrible thing if you touch him."

The king said, "If you people are not willing to punish him, then once we land I will get other people who will gladly listen to me and punish this man."

When they were about to reach the shore, Troilanga Swami placed his hand in the water. All of a sudden two shining swords appeared in his hand. They were identical, and both looked exactly like the one he had thrown into the Ganges. Everybody was astonished. The Master said to the king, "O King, now find the one that belonged to you."

The king was totally nonplussed. He did not know which sword was actually his. Then Troilanga Swami said to him, "You fool, you do not know which one belongs to you? You do not know your own possession?" Then he threw away the one that was not the king's and said, "In this world nothing will remain with you. When you die, everything you have will have to remain here. To the Real in you I say, 'Do not live in the world of enjoyment. Remain in the world of aspiration. Remain in the world of light, peace and bliss. You are a king, but you are a fool as well. Be wise. Only then will you have true happiness in life. Be spiritually wise!' "

It is not a difficult task
To be the torch-bearers
Of a new creation.
Start right from this moment
By intensifying your aspiration-life.

Start Where You Are

To follow any spiritual path, you have to have some aspiration. But if you have to wait for this dynamic and spiritual energy, then you will never start your journey. If you really want the spiritual life, start from wherever you are. If you have limited energy, if your aspiration is insignificant, go deep within. You will get to the Inner Well, the Source of aspiration.

You cannot become a multimillionaire overnight. You have to start with a penny. Similarly, if you have a little aspiration, if you really care for God, then start uttering God's Name once a day, early in the morning. If you have a sincere cry for God, then you can start your spiritual journey, no matter where you are.

> *Inside each aspiration-heart,*
> *There is a lion of love*
> *That lives to roar.*

Genuine Aspiration

If you do not fulfil your desire, you are disappointed. Or even if you get the thing you wanted, still you will not be satisfied. Then you say, "No, I am not going to desire anything in a human way. I came from the Vast and I want to enter into the infinite Vast." In the life of aspiration, it is not actually your achievement that gives you satisfaction. It is your aspiration itself.

When a person asks God for some material object, only God knows whether He will give it or not, because only God knows whether it is something that person really needs. If a person gets the thing that he is crying for, it may only increase his desire. Again, if he does not get it, he will be frustrated and displeased with God. God has to decide whether it is best that he get the thing or not. But if you are a sincere seeker, if you pray to God or meditate on God for peace, light or bliss, even if He does not grant it to you the way you want, you will still be satisfied, for you will still have inner joy and inner peace. You will simply say, "He knows best. Perhaps I am not ready. That is why He is not giving me what I asked for. But He will give it to me the day I am ready."

How can you know whether your aspiration is genuine? There is an inner joy, an inner bliss, right in the inmost recesses of your heart. You may get some mental and vital joy just because you are practising the spiritual life. But the real inner joy you get only when your aspiration is true and genuine. When you have inner joy, you see and feel that you are consciously sitting and growing in the Lap of God. The more you live in the world of higher aspiration, the more convincing will be your feeling of oneness with God. When you become consciously one with God, at that time He will stand right in front of you even when you are doing the most ordinary things.

> *The beauty*
> *Of a sincere aspiration*
> *And the purity*
> *Of a sincere dedication*
> *Can and will*
> *Definitely take the seeker*
> *To his Source immortal.*

Expect Only From God

Expectation creates frustration. This moment a fleeting desire is satisfied, but the next moment another desire is frustrated. If you really want to be happy, then you must not expect anything from the world. You have to expect only from God. Even from Him, today you will expect something and tomorrow, if you do not get it, you may feel frustrated. You do have a right to expect everything from God, but the choice hour has to be fixed by God Himself.

One day a close disciple of a great spiritual Master came to the Master and said, "Master, you have been telling me not to expect anything from my life, but to expect everything only from God. I do have faith in God, but unless and until I have seen Him face to face, how can I expect anything from Him? If I see a person, I may expect something from him, but if I do not see him, what can I expect from him? I see my own limbs, and just because I see them, I feel that I can ask them for a favour. But in the case of God, since I do not see Him, how can I expect anything from Him?"

The Master said, "My child, it is true that you have not seen God, but I wish to tell you that there are many things you get which do not actually come from an action of your hands, or eyes, or any part of your body. These things do occur, even though you do not see any outer cause or endeavour made by a person known to you. They come in God's own Way, which is far beyond your imagination."

"Master, that is true. But I must say that very often when I expect something from God, my expectations are not fulfilled."

The Master said, "When you expect something from yourself, do your expectations meet with fulfilment all the time?"

"No, Master."

"If you cannot satisfy all that you expect of yourself, why do you expect God to satisfy all that you expect of Him? Someone expects something because he has set a goal for himself or he has some destination in mind, and either he pulls that destination into himself or he pushes himself to that destination. But his own efforts are not always enough to give him success. There is a higher force, which is called Grace, the Compassion of God. When the Compassion descends from Above, there is nothing you cannot expect from your life. When divine Compassion descends, if you have a divine expectation, it is certain to be fulfilled.

"Again, in the beginning of his journey, a seeker may aim at a lower goal because he is not yet aware of his higher capacity, or because he is not freed from his desires. If the individual does not have real, sincere aspiration, if he is not a genuine seeker, then God may just give him what he consciously wants and expects. But if he prays and meditates soulfully, because God sees his sincerity and potentiality, God will not want him to reach the lesser goal. God is keeping an infinitely higher goal ready for him.

"In the beginning your expectation may be an iota of light, but God is preparing you so that He can give you an infinite expanse of light. In the beginning you may try to get just a drop of nectar; you may feel that that is enough. But God wants to feed you a very large quantity of nectar. So when you are totally sincere in your spiritual life, if you have a lesser goal, God may deny it to you because He has kept the highest Goal for you. But because you do not see the highest Goal, you feel that God is unkind to you and does not care for you."

"What is a lower or lesser goal?" the disciple asked.

"Let me give you an example," replied the Master. "I used to want to become a ticket checker on a train. When I was a child and the ticket checker came by and asked for the tickets, I was so fascinated by his movements and gestures that I wanted to become just like him. Now, look! I have become a spiritual Master. This is an infinitely greater achievement. God did not allow me to achieve the lesser goal.

"I also once wanted to become a great athlete, a very fast runner, but God wanted something else. He wanted me to become a very fast runner not in the outer life, but in the inner life. The name, fame and achievement of the athlete who is a champion runner in the outer life last only for a few years. He inspires young people, true, but the inspiration he offers is nothing compared with the inspiration that the inner champion, the spiritual Master, offers. When a Master inspires someone, that person's consciousness is elevated, and the person goes one step further towards the highest Goal. The ultimate

Goal can eventually be reached with the help of a Master's inspiration and aspiration."

The disciple said, "But Master, even when I expect the highest goal from God – peace, light and bliss in infinite measure – even then my expectations are not fulfilled."

"My son, when you expect peace, light and bliss from God, that means you have set yourself a very high goal. You may feel that what you have received is only a tiny drop, while the thing that you are still expecting is an infinite ocean. But when God gives you only a drop, it is because He feels that even this tiny drop may be too much for you. Gradually God increases your capacity, and there will come a time when you will be able to receive a big drop. And finally you will be able to receive the ocean itself.

"If you expect something from God but do not get it, rest assured that God has a very good and legitimate reason for not giving it to you. It is because He will give you something far better in the future. Also, He will tell you the reason why He is denying you. If He does not fulfil your expectation, He offers you light. Through that light, He makes it clear to you why He is not giving you what you expect. Again, if He gives you what you want immediately, then also He will tell you the reason you are getting it now. So, my child, if you really want to expect something, expect not from yourself, not from anybody else, but only from God.

"The fulfilment of expectation is at once a human necessity and a divine satisfaction. But this fulfilment takes place in a divine way only when we surrender our will to God's Will. Otherwise we shall pray to God, meditate on God, worship God and try to please God with the wrong kind of expectation. Because we have prayed for eight hours, we shall expect God to give us a smile. If we expect from God in a divine way, Reality will loom large in us and, with this Reality, we will be able to go to our highest transcendental Goal."

Today is the day
God wants me to sit beside Him
On His Golden Throne
And not in front of Him.

Opening Of The Perfection-Lotus

A farmer sows thousands of seeds, but perhaps only a few hundred of the seeds ever germinate. He offers equal concern while he is throwing the seeds, but the seed itself must have some power of receptivity. Like this, God is giving what He has: His Light. But each individual has to feel the necessity of receiving it. One person is hungry and somebody else is not. If one person has an insatiable hunger and someone else is satisfied with only a little, naturally the former will accept more.

Aspiration and receptivity go together; they are like two friends. When you aspire, at that time receptivity comes and shakes hands with you. And when you are receptive, aspiration feels that in you it has found a home. If we aspire sincerely, then the higher forces are all the time descending and can enter into us properly. If we do not aspire, then the doors are all closed. Let us say that the divine Grace wants to descend into us. Now naturally the Grace cannot descend, since our heart-door we have kept closed. But when we sincerely aspire, we open up the heart, mind, vital and every other part of our being. Aspiration is going up and the doors are all open, so the divine Grace is descending into us. We allow it to descend fully into us without being hampered.

The heart, the mind, the vital and the body-consciousness need the capacity to do the right thing and grow into the right thing. If we sincerely aspire, then our aspiration will significantly increase our capacity in every part of our existence. Inside our aspiration, our perfection is glowing and growing. Sincere aspiration means the

77

opening of the perfection-lotus. A lotus has many petals. Each time we aspire most soulfully, one petal of the lotus blooms. And when one petal blossoms, it means perfection is increasing in the entire lotus.

Every morning
My Lord Supreme enters into
My heart-nest
Smiling and dancing
With a lotus in His Hand.

Ways To Rekindle The Aspiration-Flame

At times your aspiration, before it reaches its Goal, ceases. Your heart's mounting flame rises upward, but there are a few stops and breaks. First of all, I would like to tell you that you are not alone. All spiritual aspirants, with no exception, have gone through these ups and downs in their spiritual life. Sometimes we feel that we are walking through beautiful green forests and meadows. But then we find ourselves walking through deserts in scorching heat. When we cross this barren, empty desert, we feel that there is no aspiration. We have to feel that aspiration is there, although right now we seem to be on an endless journey.

When this happens to you, how can you escape from this desert? There are several ways. Let us say that every day your appointed time for meditation is six o'clock in the morning. But for the past two days you have been unable to go deep within or to meditate sincerely, and now you are frustrated. At that time you should choose a spiritual book written by a realised soul or by a devotee who is full of devotion. Then, while reading the book, you will see your whole body become a flood of tears, tears of delight. To read a book written by a spiritual Master or devotee at the time of a dry period in your spiritual life is one of the most effective ways of returning to the zenith of your spiritual aspiration.

But what if you do not have a book written by an illumined soul or a devotee? The second method is to go immediately and mix with other sincere seekers. With them you will have spiritual conversations. You will appreciate how God has shown you such Love, Concern and Compassion. In the beginning you may feel that you are such a hypocrite in saying, "Oh, I am now in a miserable condition and I am appreciating God." But you will see that if you just start appreciating the Supreme, immediately you will shed tears. These tears come directly from your soul. And your soul will then unite you again with your highest aspiration.

Another method is to keep a spiritual diary. During your spiritual journey, you can write down notes of your soul-illumining experiences, visions and inner feelings. Today you are in despair, in darkest night. But two months ago you were in the brightest light. You had a wonderful experience. You saw that Krishna was playing the flute right in front of you, or your whole existence became a sea of delight. Whenever you have good, high, elevating experiences, please write them down in your diary. As soon as you read it, your inner being will respond to the highest experiences you had two months ago.

If we can recollect our highest and deepest experiences at the moment we are frustrated or in despair, then we will get immediate relief. Immediately the soul's joy will drive away our despondent feelings.

When all else fails,
Try to smile.
To your great surprise,
You will succeed.

The Aspiration-Hero

If you have true aspiration and genuine love for God, if you want to go far, farther, farthest, then embark on the inner path. Your soul's inner awakening will compel your body, vital, mind and heart to follow you devotedly.

You can get courage from your aspiration if you can make yourself feel that you are a chosen hero-instrument of the Supreme. The very word "hero", the very concept of heroism, can grant you courage. Again, aspiration itself is courage. Only a brave person can aspire. As a seeker you have to feel that you have a most significant task to perform. When you feel this, you will go one step within. What is the message that you will receive? From within yourself, the answer will come that you have to become a most perfect instrument and a unique messenger of Light and Truth.

Just because we know
That we are not perfect,
We follow a spiritual path
To try to become perfect.
Otherwise, there is no necessity
Of our following the spiritual life.

Dedication

No more tomorrows.
No more todays.
It is now, at this very moment,
That I shall become a divinely good
And supremely chosen instrument
Of my Lord Supreme.

When we love God, naturally we want to devote ourselves to Him. Divine devotion is a soul-stirring emotion that dynamically permeates our entire consciousness. Divine devotion is adoration – the spontaneous delight that springs from the deepest recesses of our heart. In devotion there is a tremendous intimacy – a very intimate concern and feeling of inseparable oneness between the seeker and God.

Human devotion is nothing but unrecognised attachment. We say that we are devoted to someone or to something, but if we go deep within, we discover that this feeling is nothing but our attachment to that individual or to that cause. But divine devotion is totally different. Divine devotion is dedication to a higher purpose, to a higher way of life, to an ideal or goal. It grows out of our promise to our inner being to manifest our inner divinity here on earth. Divine devotion is our oneness-cry for the higher reality, our feeling that there is a purpose for our lives and our need to establish our deepest oneness with that purpose. It helps us to grow into the infinite Consciousness.

If we have real devotion to the light within us, at that time we enter into a higher world to bring down peace, light and bliss from Above and bring to the fore our own inner divinity. We devote

81

ourselves wholeheartedly to the supreme Cause. In divine devotion we always feel the necessity of offering our very existence to the One whom we really and eternally love, who is God. Since God is our own highest and most illumined Reality, it is easy to devote our existence to Him. When we devote ourselves to the Supreme, to the Inner Pilot, we feel boundless satisfaction. Then, if we love God inside each human being, we try to serve Him in everyone. We offer our dedicated devotion to the divinity within humanity.

God is like a tree. The tree looks beautiful only if it has many branches, leaves and fruit. Otherwise, if we see a tree that has only the trunk, we will not appreciate it. God is the tree with all its branches and leaves. He is one but, at the same time, He is many. When we meditate in silence, with tears of devotion, that is one form of meditation. Then, when we try to dedicate ourselves to the rest of the world, we are doing another form of meditation that is called manifestation. At that time we are serving the divinity in humanity.

My service to humanity
Is my real opportunity
To prove my genuine love
For God and God alone.

Dedicated Action

Devotion is something very intense, especially if it is used in a spiritual way. It is the divine intensity and the supreme dynamism in love. Devotion expresses itself in dedicated action – action that is inspired by the seeker's inner being. A spiritual person has found his work. His work is selfless service. His work is dedicated action.

Action is conquering life's untold miseries and teeming limitations. Action is transforming life's devouring imperfection into glowing perfection. Action is something infinitely deeper and higher than the mere survival of physical existence. Action is the secret supreme that enables us to enter into the Life Eternal.

Someone who has not consciously accepted the spiritual life may consider action a necessary evil. But to a spiritual person, action is a divine blessing. To him, God-realisation is not enough. His is the heart that cries for God's all-fulfilling manifestation. God says that a person of divine action is the ideal hero. This ideal hero manifests God here on earth.

Meditation is the key to enter the divine world. Early in the morning we have to meditate. But it is not enough just to cry inwardly; when our meditation is over, our life must be an expression of that inner cry. If, during meditation, we love the world but hate it as soon as our meditation is over, then that is not a good meditation. Our meditation must follow us when we enter into the hustle and bustle of life and inspire us to offer our capacity.

All seekers of the Absolute Supreme
Have the sacred responsibility
Of universal fraternity.

God Is The Doer

According to Indian philosophy, there are three principal paths that lead to God-realisation: the path of love and devotion, or bhakti yoga; the path of knowledge, or jnana yoga; and the path of selfless service, or karma yoga. "Karma" is a Sanskrit word which means action. Karma yoga is action undertaken for the sake of the Supreme.

When we practise karma yoga, we try to make all our work a true dedicated service to the Supreme. In our day-to-day life, duty is something unpleasant, demanding and discouraging. When we are reminded of our duty, we lose all our spontaneous inner joy; we feel miserable. We feel that we could have used our life-energy for a better purpose. Simply because we do our work with our ego, pride and vanity, duty is painful, tedious and monotonous. Duty is pleasant, encouraging and inspiring when we do it for God's sake. What we need to change is our attitude towards duty.

In general, I advise people to take their work, whatever it may be, as dedicated service. Everyone needs money. If we go to the grocery store with only our aspiration, the owner will not give us any food. If we offer to give him light, peace and bliss in exchange for food, he will just laugh. Money is necessary for us. But when we work, we have to know that we are working for a special purpose: to keep our body on earth and to become a divine instrument.

If you are doing something unpleasant or boring and are not getting any joy, or if your work does not seem rewarding, you are bound to feel miserable if you think that it is you performing the action. But if you feel that God, the Inner Pilot, is doing it in and through you, and that you are just His instrument, then you will lose your unconscious attachment to your work and get joy from what you are doing. If you feel that Somebody else is acting in and through you, then you will find abundant peace in the day-to-day activities that now seem unpleasant to you. At that time the burden of responsibility, the tension and the disheartening thoughts and ideas that plague your mind will leave you.

In ordinary work, people immediately expect something in return; they expect success or fortune or advancement. But when someone practises karma yoga, he works most devotedly and soulfully without caring for the result. He knows that the result will come in the form of either success or failure; he accepts both as an experience. Also, he feels that this experience is not actually his; it is the experience of God. When the seeker goes deep within, he sees that God Himself is the doer, the work and the result. When the seeker is just a beginner, he feels that God is the giver and he is the receiver. But when he becomes advanced, he feels that God Himself is always acting and experiencing Himself in and through him.

"Thou hast the right to act, but claim not the fruits thereof." Lord Krishna has given this message in the Bhagavad Gita, the Song Celestial. If we can see God's Presence in each action, then see the action itself as God, and later the result – success or failure – as God, and finally the doer of the action as God, then all our problems are over.

I am singing and dancing
Because my Lord took care of
The planning.

Work: The Prayer Of The Body

You have to know that you can feel God's Presence in anything you do. When you are eating, you can feel that the food is God. While you are feeding your child, feel that you are not feeding him but rather the God within him. While you are talking to someone, feel that you are talking to the divinity in him. If you can be conscious of God while you are doing something, then you can feel that God has entered into your activity. Then whatever you are doing is with God and for God. If you can keep your consciousness high and maintain peace of mind while working, then your work itself is a true form of meditation.

Right now, when you are working, you may not think of God, or you may not feel the reality of God. You see physical work as just work. But if you can see work as an opportunity to express your capacity, or to reveal your goodness, your divinity, then most certainly you are working for God at that time. Please feel that everything you do is dedicated service. In that way, you will not feel that you are wasting your time.

If you can feel that you are doing something because you have been asked to do it from within, then you will have the greatest joy. You are not the doer; you are only a dedicated instrument serving a higher Reality. If you can feel this, then you will get joy no matter what you do. Even if you are doing something mechanical or something that is absolutely uninspiring, you will get the greatest joy, because you are serving a higher cause.

If you wish to be constantly helped and guided by the Supreme, please remind yourself of Him in the morning, as soon as you get up. Then think of the things that you do daily. You do twenty, thirty or forty things each day. Before you do each thing, you should try to remember the Supreme. Just before you are about to eat, think of the Supreme. After you have spoken with someone and you are just about to speak with somebody else, meditate for a minute. And if you see that you do not have the time, then try to meditate as soon as you are free. Each time you change your activity, meditate on the Supreme for just a minute. Your meditation should be soulful and not mechanical.

You have to feel that work, if you do it devotedly, is the prayer of the body. When you are doing even the most minor, insignificant act, such as sharpening your pencil, you should feel that the capacity you have for sharpening the pencil, for utilising your hands to hold it, has come directly from God. When you dedicate all your outer actions to God, this capacity you are giving directly back to God. When you do this for minor activities, immediately you see that God gives you infinitely more power when you enter into more com-plicated, more meaningful, more purposeful activities. Whatever you do, please try to think that you are given the opportunity to do that by God; think that you are doing something which is ultimately leading you towards your realisation.

The devotion-musician in me
Is all ready to play
God's Song of Love
Upon my heart-strings
In the New Millennium.

A Time For Everything

During action, the best way to meditate is to remember to offer yourself, the action, and the result of the action to the Supreme. You need not go to your shrine and meditate on God with tears of devotion if at that very moment you have something most important to do in the outer world.

Once there was a king who needed a very, very good worker to do some special tasks in the palace. His minister found the perfect worker. This worker was very sincere, very nice-looking, very honest and so forth. But he had one bad habit: he used to come to work late. The king scolded the minister: "What kind of man is he? He is coming late to work every day. Does he not value his job in the palace?"

The minister was very embarrassed. He went to see the worker and said, "I got you the job and told the king that you were such a nice man and a good worker. Why are you behaving in this way? Why do you come late to work every day? How can you justify it?"

The man replied, "Early in the morning I go to the temple, and there I praise God. I sing God's Glory for hours and hours. That is why I arrive late."

The minister said, "This is what you do? Then when you come to the palace, why do you not sing the king's glory?"

The following day the fellow came to work and started singing the king's glory. He was extolling the king and praising him to the skies. The king observed the worker for some time. At first he was amused.

Then after half an hour or forty-five minutes the worker was still going on and on with endless singing. He was not working at all. Then the king became exasperated. He gave the man a slap and demanded, "What are you doing?"

The man said, "What can I do? The minister asked me to sing your glory."

Then the minister was summoned. The king asked him, "Why did you tell this worker to sing my glory?"

The minister said, "He told me he comes late each day because he sings God's Glory in the temple. I told him that if he came and sang your glory for a little while, you would be pleased. But I did not think that he would not work at all."

The worker said in his own defence, "God created me. That is why I go to the temple every day and sing God's praises."

The minister said, "God created you, and God also wants you to live on earth, to work honestly. By praising God constantly, how will you be able to support yourself? If you wanted to praise God all day long, why did you accept this job? There is a time for everything. If you go to the temple early in the morning, you can praise God before you come to work. Then you will come to the palace punctually and work here. At the end of the day, you will take your salary and buy what you need. In this way, everything will have its proper time. Come to work on time. Then after finishing your work here, you can again go to the temple. But in the meantime you must work."

The minister was right. The following day the worker arrived at the palace on time. He had already gone to the temple and offered his praises to God. Then he came to work because he was getting money from the king. He sang the king's praises for a short time, and then he started working.

The king was pleased with this worker and the minister was pleased with him. God was also pleased with him because he was doing the right thing.

To change the world around you,
Give the world
What you have
And serve the world
With what you are.

Seeing The Divine In Ourselves And Others

When we feel not only the divinity within ourselves, but also within others, we can feel our oneness with the Supreme, the Source. One way to feel our oneness with others is to feel that we are everything. But then we may come to think that we are superior to everyone, and that will only ruin our purpose. If we feel that only we possess divinity, whereas others possess undivine forces, then immediately there will be a clash. But if we feel, while mixing with others, that we are of the Source, then we shall try also to see the divine in others. When we feel that we are divine, it is absolutely true. At the same time we have to feel that others are also divine, equally divine.

While we are praying at home, we see and feel God; God is ours. After our meditation we come out of the heart and enter into the mind. The moment we come out of our house and look around at others, we do not try to see God inside them. Then we separate ourselves from others and we see them as undivine. Instead, when we come out into the world, if we can bring with us the divinity that we saw and felt during our meditation at home, and if we try to see the same divinity in others, then there is no feeling of separation. And if we see in others what we feel inside ourselves, then we shall never miss God's Presence. We shall never lose our feeling of oneness with God.

If God is your only Friend,
You are bound to see God
In everybody.

89

Serving God Inside Everybody

When you pray and meditate you feel that God is inside everybody, that He is a living Reality. You know that God is everywhere and in everything, true. But when you pray and meditate, this mental belief becomes a real, living truth to you. At that time you consciously serve people precisely because you know and feel that God is inside them.

If you feel that you have some capacity to inspire or help someone, even though you do not see God's Presence inside that person, then you are only aggrandising your ego by letting it tell you that you have more inner wealth than the other person. If you are doing something and at the same time feeling God's Presence in the work itself, then that dedication is meditation. The timing of each action is also significant. If it is God's Will that the person seeking help should receive aid at that time and through you, then you will be guided to do so. The best thing is to see if you are getting an inner command to help others.

Suppose you do not know what the truth is, but you have sincere concern for someone. You want to help him, but you do not know what you are going to say. At that time do not form any idea of how to help him or what you will tell him. Make your mind an empty vessel. Then let the vessel be filled with God's Light and God's Wisdom, and share it.

We have to be careful when we use the term "help". Only the Inner Pilot can help us, guide us and mould us. True service is rendered with humility. When we serve soulfully, then there can be no pride, because we do not feel superior. We feel we are serving the Supreme in others. Each human being houses a few good qualities and a few bad qualities. If we offer our own good qualities to the good qualities in others, these qualities become most powerful. Then it is like two people in a tug-of-war against ignorance; in this case, naturally, the divine will win.

When your good qualities
Go and touch others,
Their good qualities come forward
To receive from you.

The Power Of Love

If we want to strengthen our devotion to a cause, to our Master, to our own spiritual life or to God, then we have to feel the utmost necessity of love. If there is no love – inner love, divine love – then there can be no devotion.

When we love someone, we try to spend our precious time with or thinking about that particular person. In the spiritual life, too, if we love God, then naturally we will have the inner urge to offer our pure love to Him and to devote ourselves to Him. Even human love freely offers itself to please the loved one. In the spiritual life, this self-offering has to be far more intense. We should be ready to give all that we have and all that we are.

If we want to strengthen our devotion, we can do it in abundant measure if we have the inner strength, capacity or willingness to say, "I love God for God's sake. Him to please in His own Way, I exist on earth." If this is our will, if this is what we want from life, then automatically God's adamantine Protection, unconditional Concern and unconditional Compassion will descend on us. At that time our devotion to God or to any divine cause is bound to be strengthened in abundant measure. The easiest and most effective way to please God is by constant and unconditional self-offering. Let us try. We shall, without fail, succeed.

Take just one positive step.
Every day say:
"My heart is of God
And my life is for God."

Surrender

Two are the darlings of Heaven:
Light and Delight.
Two are the darlings of earth:
Cry and surrender.
Two are the darlings of God:
You and I.
But you must never breathe
This secret supreme to anyone.

Surrender is a spiritual miracle. It teaches us how to see God with our eyes closed; how to talk to God with our mouth shut. Surrender means spontaneous joy. In life, everything may fail us, but not surrender. God may, at times, play hide-and-seek with the seeker's other divine qualities, but never with His devotee's genuine surrender.

When an aspirant is totally surrendered to God's Will, he will feel all joy in his heart and he will live in constant joy. He will not be able to account for it or give any meaning to it. Early in the morning, when he first gets up, he will get a very sweet feeling or sensation. If he touches a wall, he will get joy; if he touches a mirror, he will also get joy. If a taxi-cab goes by, he will see intense joy in the driver, even in the cab itself. His own joy will enter into everything he sees, and it will pervade everything.

In human surrender we notice tremendous force; we feel that we are under compulsion – as in the surrender of the slave to the master. The slave surrenders unwillingly; he is afraid that his master may punish him. He surrenders out of fear. But divine surrender to God's Will is a dedicated, devoted and loving surrender; there is no compulsion.

In spiritual surrender, the finite consciously enters into the Infinite. Without surrendering, we will not know that we are infinite, eternal and immortal. Surrender means becoming consciously one with our real Self, our infinite Self. At that time we do not lose our own finite individuality; instead, we become in addition the possessor of divine Infinity. Our imperfect nature becomes totally one with our perfect nature.

> *When I think of surrendering myself*
> *Unconditionally to my Lord Supreme,*
> *The wings of Heaven start singing*
> *And dancing.*

Claiming God As Our Own

When we offer our existence to God, we have the feeling of oneness between father or mother and child. The little child feels that what his parents have, he also has. He is only three years old, but he says, "I have a car." He does not say, "My father has a car." He will simply say, "It is my car, our car." We need to change our understanding of our relationship with God. If He has peace, then we have every right to claim this peace as our own. Because God is our Father, our Mother, we can have that kind of feeling. If we feel that we are God's slaves and that we have to do everything for Him, then we will have no inner feeling, no assurance, no guarantee that He will please us. But if we have the feeling of oneness between father or mother and child, there is no problem, because we know that what the mother or father has, the child has every right to claim as his very own.

If you remain inside God's Consciousness,
You will see God
As your Father and Mother,
Your Sister and Brother,
Your Friend, Your All.

The Path Of The Heart

If we follow the path of the heart, there is a constant flow of love and oneness. Even if we feel that we have not achieved anything, but someone else has achieved much, our heart will make us feel that his achievement is ours, since he is our brother. In the spiritual world, we came from the same Eternal Father, so why should there be any separation between us?

When the heart accepts something, it lasts forever. If we love someone, if that love comes from the very depths of our heart, no matter what the person does, we shall love him. A mother's real, spontaneous love for her child is like that. The child can do anything. He can criticise the mother, insult the mother, leave the house, do anything. But the mother's heart will always remain inside the heart of the child, because the mother has established her oneness with the child's heart.

In the spiritual life also, when we follow the path of the heart, once we learn to love God, that is enough. We shall love Him no matter what happens to us. Even if He does not fulfil even one desire out of a million desires, we will not mind. We will just say, "It is up to Him to fulfil our desires or not." Since we have accepted the spiritual life, we want to encourage our aspiration, not our desire. We are trying, we are aspiring to become good, God-loving and man-fulfilling. These are our goals. We want to love the world because we feel the Presence of God inside the world and inside everyone.

There is only one life:
God's Love-Blessing
Here, there and all-where.

False Freedom And Real Freedom

People are constantly using their own whimsical will, and they feel that their will is their freedom. But there is no freedom in that will. We have to know that there are different kinds of freedom. There is human freedom and divine freedom; false freedom and real freedom.

False freedom is our constant and deliberate acceptance of ignorance and our conscious existence in ignorance. Real freedom is our conscious awareness of our inner divinity and our constant and inseparable oneness with our Inner Pilot. False freedom constantly wants to prove its capacity and sovereignty. It has a new goal every day, and it wants to discover this goal only in the desire-life. But real freedom, inner freedom, constantly wants to prove that it belongs to God and God alone. It has only one goal, and that goal is, at every moment, to be consciously aware of God and consciously manifesting God.

Each God-surrender-step
Brings us closer and closer
To God.

The Drop And The Ocean

Right now we feel that we are a tiny drop. Why? Because we have separated our existence from the mighty ocean. As long as we maintain our sense of separateness, we will not dare to enter into the ocean. If we take the theoretical approach and feel that the ocean in front of us will always remain vast, then we will always remain the drop. But when we are practical, we just dive into the ocean and become one with it. As soon as we enter into the ocean, we experience the consciousness of the ocean itself. We may swim in only one particular spot, but the consciousness of the vast ocean becomes ours.

We know that our existence here on earth is filled with imperfection, limitation and bondage. But we have another existence all our own: perfection, plenitude and infinity. When we consciously give our lower existence to our higher existence, it is the surrender of oneness to our own highest height – to the Absolute Supreme, who is our very own.

When we surrender ourselves entirely to God, on the strength of our surrender we become absolutely one with God. God stands with open arms and embraces us, saying, "Come into My Heart."

> *Be as close as possible,*
> *To be embraced*
> *By God Himself.*

The Victory Supreme

When a runner begins to run, he exerts his limbs to the limit. Then, after a few minutes, his movements become very spontaneous. When he is running the fastest, he will feel that he is not running at all. His movement becomes automatic and he feels that there is no exertion. Real surrender is like that. When we make our total unconditional surrender to God, we feel that we do nothing, absolutely nothing; we have become a mere instrument.

If you can surrender your will to the Will of the Supreme, absolute satisfaction will dawn in your life. Right now you are struggling and struggling to surrender your will to the Supreme. But, each time you make this surrender, you are gaining strength. Then, eventually, you will reach the point where even if you want to have a will that is separate from the divine Will, you will not be able to, because you will have merged with the one Will. At that point, yours will be the Victory Supreme.

> *Without God's approval,*
> *I do not make*
> *A single move.*

Let Thy Will Be Done

The Christ revealed the supreme secret when he said, "Let Thy Will be done." There cannot be any prayer higher than this. You can try to please God in your own way, and God will be pleased to some extent. But if you can please Him in His own Way, then God can think of you as His chosen instrument. The moment you make your total, unconditional surrender to God's Will, when you can say, "Let Thy Will be done," God will say, "You are ready now. I can accept you as My chosen instrument."

> *God does not care if He has*
> *Ten thousand friends or one friend*
> *On earth,*
> *As long as He has one particular friend,*
> *Whom He loves the most:*
> *Our heart's unconditional surrender*
> *To His Will supreme.*
> *As long as He has this friend,*
> *He does not need other friends.*

To Have A One-Pointed Love Of God

The first thing is to have one-pointed love for God. This is the only thing that is correct, necessary and indispensable in life. If you love God, then you are doing the right thing. Right now you are a tiny seed or a tiny plant in the spiritual life, and until you become strong, the forces in society have the ability to destroy you. Today you are a tiny plant, but tomorrow you will grow into a huge banyan tree. At that time, people can do anything with the tree and the tree will survive. They can tie twenty cows to it with a rope, but the tree is not going to fall down.

While you are loving God, He will give you the inspiration, energy and capacity to distribute your love in a pure way, a divine way, amongst your fellow travellers in the spiritual life. By loving God you will know what is best for you – what to say, how to behave, how to act. All answers will come if you feel the divine in yourself and try to become as close as possible to the divinity within you.

Lord, my Lord, I love You
Not because You have all Power,
Not because I need a special favour,
But because You are my Master-Friend
And my Supreme Love.

Part Three

The Undivine Forces

Disobedience

Disobedience means
The mind's bold refusal
To bow
To the illumined heart.

Inner obedience is a supreme virtue. When we obey the higher principles, higher laws, we love. When we love, we become. And when we become, we come to realise that we eternally are the Eternal Now.

Obedience is a forced life: this is the realisation of an unaspiring person. In the unaspiring life we feel that duty is another name for labour. Human duty begins with compulsion and very often ends in frustration. But the obedience that I wish to talk about is inner obedience. Inner obedience is the conscious recognition of one's higher life, higher reality, higher existence.

If there is inner obedience, then there is nothing that we cannot do, absolutely nothing. This obedience must be based on inner faith. If you cultivate that faith, you will soon grow into obedience. God is our Eternity's Beloved Supreme. If you have faith in what the Supreme is saying and if you continue your spiritual life in this way, this is inner obedience.

Our God-faith
Solves
All our life-problems.

To Be One With The Infinite Love

When we go deep within, we see that there is only one person who is constantly and eternally faithful to us, and that is God. From time immemorial He has been faithful to us, faithful to His creation. We obey our Inner Pilot not because He is all-powerful, not out of fear that He will punish us. We obey Him because He is all Love. He is our Love-Power, and our life needs Love-Power. Our existence wants to be one with the infinite Love. When we outwardly obey God, even out of fear, we gain something. But when we inwardly and outwardly offer our obedience to our Inner Pilot, we make the fastest progress.

A child obeys his parents. In the spiritual life we are all children; we are eternally children. We listen to the Inner Voice, the Inner Pilot, who is guiding our destiny, who is moulding and shaping us in His own Way. When a sincere seeker becomes an obedient child of God, he feels that it is his inner necessity and outer necessity that have compelled him to cry for God and become inseparably one with God's infinite Light, Peace and Bliss. He also feels that it is God's Necessity that constantly has need of his obedience. He acquires inner obedience because his human feelings are transformed into the divine life. He has developed the hunger for God-realisation; and God Himself has developed the hunger for His own manifestation. Through whom? Through the seeker, His devoted, surrendered instrument.

Our first experience is loving God. Our second experience is devoting ourselves to God. And our third experience is "Let Thy Will be done." This is the crown of divine obedience.

I know, I know,
Because I love God,
The clouds of confusion
Will disappear today.

102

I know, I know,
Because I obey God,
The skies of adversity
Will clear tomorrow.

Taking Obedience Seriously

In life we can take everything seriously; again, everything we can take lightly. But it is precisely because we have taken many, many things in life lightly right from the beginning that today our spirituality has become a most difficult task. In our spiritual life, there should be obedience at every moment.

There is no such thing as insignificant disobedience. You have to write this down on the tablet of your heart. If you think, "This is insignificant," or "That is insignificant," then the very thing which is most important in your life will come and appear right in front of you, but you will say, "Oh, this is also not important." Gradually you will see that everything in your life you are taking lightly.

Be wise!
You must overcome
All your difficulties,
Not try to escape from them.
For there is no such thing
As escape.

Pride: Self-Destruction's Next-Door Neighbour

When we treasure pride, we do not see that self-destruction is fast approaching us. In the spiritual life, pride is an enemy. Pride immediately separates us. Pride always belittles others' capacities. Pride does not want anybody else to go higher.

A man can be very insincere, very impure in his own life, but he can have love for others. He can have feelings, true feelings. But, when pride comes, it never allows us to identify ourselves with others. Pride always likes separation, separation, separation. If you have other unfortunate qualities – for example, jealousy, insecurity, impurity, insincerity – somehow you will be able to deal with them. But if you develop pride in any way, then self-destruction is next door. You will be able to handle all your other bad qualities, but do not nourish or feed your pride in any way. God gave you your achievements. In the twinkling of an eye, He can take away your achievements.

Again, you are grateful to the Supreme, for He has given you many wonderful capacities. If you show your gratitude, God will be pleased with you, and then God may intervene between you and your pride and say, "Be grateful to Me. Again, be kind to others. I gave you the capacity."

As You Sow, So Shall You Reap

Now, if we do something wrong, we have to know that either today or tomorrow, either in the physical world or in the inner world, we will receive the result of it. Again, if we do something good, if we pray, if we meditate, if we do divine things, there too we will get the result. It is absolutely true that "as you sow, so shall you reap."

The law of karma, the law of action and reaction, can be nullified only when the divine Grace descends. But if God's Grace does not descend on the individual who has committed a mistake, naturally he has to pay the penalty for his misdeed. There is no such thing as escape. I cannot go on doing something undivine and feel that God, the Cosmic Law, will forgive me. I have done something today. The next moment I will get the result, or it may be months later or perhaps years later. But if I have done something wrong and I really have repentance, if I really do not do it again, if I shed bitter tears and God sees a soulful cry within my heart, naturally He will forgive me. He will also give me the necessary strength not to commit the same mistake again.

Suppose you, as a child, have hurt someone, and your father is right beside you when you do it. Then suppose the other child comes to strike you because you have done something wrong to him. Your father, since he is strongest, in spite of knowing that you were wrong, may not allow this. Your father has the strength. Similarly, in your inner life, suppose you have done something wrong and you cry to God. He has the power to nullify your mistake. Your ignorant and wrong action can be forgiven by God's Grace, and you can be saved and illumined by God the Eternal Father.

An unconditionally surrendered seeker
Is far beyond
All the mountains of problems.

The Master's Compassion

A spiritual Master has the heart of a real mother. When the Master sees that somebody is about to be punished for his wrong karma, if the Master wants and if it is the Will of God, immediately he will take the pain inside himself. Or he can take the pain and immediately throw it into the universe.

If the mother knows that her child has done something wrong and will be punished, she says, "O God, let me suffer on my child's behalf." If the child is divine, loving and sincere, when he sees his mother suffering, he says, "I deserved this suffering, but my mother is suffering on my behalf. She has all love for me. Let me not cause her more suffering. Let me not do this again."

The Master sees that some of his disciples have sincerely accepted the spiritual life, but while following it, sometimes they enter into the world of temptation and are captured. He says, "Since you are serving God, or you are trying to please God in various ways, let me help you so that you do not have to suffer." This is sheer divine compassion.

> *There are only two things*
> *To remember:*
> *I must never give up;*
> *God is watching me.*

Dealing With Past Mistakes

On the whole, we are carrying the past inside us. But I always say "the past is dust", because the past has not made you what you want to be. Your attitude should be that the past is buried in oblivion. If you cherish the idea of guilt, you are being sincere, but this sincerity does not help. Yes, you have done something wrong, but by having a guilty conscience you do not get light or wisdom.

If you have used one minute for a wrong purpose, use the following minute for a divine purpose. When you do not think of the previous minute, when you did something wrong, then what happens? Your positive strength, the will-power you have used to do the right thing, will then have its power in entirety. Try to bring forward this full power in the following minute and nullify the previous mistake. Think, "I am a hero; I am ready to face the consequences. If I have done something wrong, then I have the capacity to do the right thing."

Every second a seeker can start over,
For his life's mistakes
Are initial drafts
And not the final version.

In The Garden Of God's Heart

The aspiration-life is the life of inner obedience. Obedience is self-giving, the offering of our unlit consciousness to our illumined consciousness. Let us take the unlit in us as our feet; and let us call the illumined consciousness in us our head. The feet and the head have to establish an inseparable oneness. Here it is not a question of obedience; it is necessity. When an individual wants to run very fast, he needs tremendous concentration-power from his mind and his heart. The mind and heart will come to help the feet. Heart, mind and feet are all running towards one goal: that is, conscious expansion of our existence. When one part of the being needs special attention, another part comes to its rescue, and together they reach the goal.

There is one most important thing in the spiritual life, and that most important thing is: God first and God last. We will start our journey with God, we will end our journey with God, and in between God will be there, too. In the Garden of God's Heart, a beautiful rose with celestial fragrance blossoms each time we obey our Inner Pilot.

God created you for only two purposes.
One is to be true to Him
And the other is to be true to yourself.

Insecurity

You do not have to prove
God's Love for you.
Just feel that you live
Only for God's Love.

Our conception of security is an achievement or a possession on the physical plane, vital plane or mental plane, but an abiding sense of security can never come from possession or from achievement. In the unaspiring life there is no such thing as security. Nobody can be secure in his own life or in the lives of others. Here on earth when we want to establish security in our own capacities and talents, we come to realise that it is impossible. Then we become a perfect slave to someone else in order to gain security.

We ourselves may cherish insecurity within us. It is like the child who does not know the difference between sand and milk. If you put both in front of him, then he may eat the sand. We may feel that insecurity is a most delicious fruit, but when it is compared with security, with inner joy and confidence, it is nothing. Once we have got real confidence, inner confidence, we can make the comparison and see the difference.

No matter how powerful, how rich or how wise we are, we may not feel totally secure. Why? Precisely because we have not established oneness with other individuals. And there cannot be total oneness, constant, eternal and inseparable oneness, unless and until we have established our oneness with the Supreme. We have to know that the Supreme is all security. If we go deep within, then we will be able to feel secure in our Source.

The sweetest and the richest
Of all occupations
Is when I think of God
And I feel God
As my Eternity's own,
Very own.

Going To The Highest

Two village zamindars, or village chiefs, had a quarrel and then started fighting. They brought their supporters to join the fight, and on both sides people were very badly injured. Finally everyone left the place, near a forest, except one of the two zamindars. He was so badly hurt that he was unconscious. His people all left because they did not want to be beaten by the other side. They left this zamindar alone and senseless. Nobody came to help him.

In the forest there lived a hermit. The hermit came out of the forest and started moving around. Suddenly he saw the man lying down, practically dead. He brought water for the man, fanned him and washed his face. Finally he revived the zamindar. The zamindar said to the hermit, "Please, please take something from me. If you come to my house, I will give you something."

The hermit said, "I am a hermit. I have everything, absolutely everything. I have the sun, I have the moon, I have fruits to eat. I do not need anything at all."

The zamindar said, "My pride is hurt. I took an oath that in this lifetime I would never be indebted to anybody. I said that I would only give and give, and I would not owe anybody anything. You are a hermit. You have nothing, like a beggar. I am a zamindar. I am so rich. You have to come to my place. I will give you whatever you want so that your poverty will disappear."

The hermit said, "No, no, no, I do not need anything."

The zamindar said, "But I am indebted to you."

Then the hermit said, "All right. In the future, if I need any help, I will come to you."

The zamindar begged him, "Please, please, you must come now. Otherwise I will remain indebted to you. I do not want that. My pride will be hurt. I am so rich. My people, my children, my friends, my guards – all have left me. They betrayed me because they were being beaten by the enemy. Now you have come here to rescue me. I am so grateful to you."

The hermit said, "When I am in need, I will come to you."

The zamindar was proud, but he was a good man who really wanted to help the hermit. A few years later when the hermit became very, very old, he started suffering from this disease and that disease. Then he remembered that the zamindar had promised to help him, so he went to the zamindar's place. The guard, who knew that the zamindar had once upon a time been helped by the hermit, said, "He is now taking a bath. After that, he will come and see you."

The hermit waited near the zamindar's meditation room. After finishing his bath, the zamindar went to his meditation room and, with folded hands, knelt down and started praying to God, "Give me more wealth, give me more name, give me more fame! Please give me more people, more strength." For all these things he started praying.

The hermit said to himself, "I came here to beg this zamindar to give me some medicine or to find a doctor to cure me. Now I see that he is begging God to give him this and that. I have only one desire: for my disease to be cured. He has so many desires!"

The hermit got up to leave. The zamindar came out of his meditation room and asked the guard, "What did he want?" Then the zamindar saw that it was the hermit. He started running after the hermit saying, "Why are you going away? You did me such a big favour when I was dying, when I was practically dead. Now you have come to my place, and I am so happy. Please, please, please tell me what you want!"

The hermit said, "No, I will not ask you for anything."

The zamindar said, "You came here, and I still owe you so much. Do you want me to remain indebted to you all my life? If you take my help, I will be so happy and so grateful."

The hermit said, "You have already helped me."

The zamindar said, "How could I have helped you? You have not taken anything from me."

The hermit said, "Look, I pray to God every day for my illumination. Here I am seeing that you are also praying to God for what you need. You have taught me that there is only one Person who can give us what we need. You have everything: name, fame, money and property. But you have gone to the one Person who is infinitely richer and stronger than you for help. I came to you, but you gave me the lesson that you are nobody in comparison to God. You have taught me to go to the Highest.

"You do not owe me anything, because you have given me the real illumination: always, for everything, we have to go to God. To cure my disease I am going to God. You have everything, but you still need more things from God for your fulfilment. In my case, I have been praying for so many years, and I should have realised this. But this lesson I got from you, so you do not owe me anything. I helped you, true, but now you have illumined me. Both of us are equal."

Someone infinitely wiser than you
Is waiting at your mind's door.
Someone infinitely purer than you
Is waiting at your heart's door.
Someone infinitely more self-giving than you
Is waiting at your life's door.
Welcome Him.

Give Him the opportunity
To do everything through you.
Needless to say,
He will do everything for you
With utmost joy.

Protection-Prayers

There are both inner attacks and outer attacks. We see only outer attacks. Outwardly we see that some calamity has taken place and somebody is a victim. But inner attacks always come before outer attacks; anything that happens outwardly has its seed in the inner world. At every moment undivine thoughts are attacking us; if it is not somebody else's wrong thoughts, then it is our own. We must pray to God to protect us, not only from others but also from ourselves. If we pray to God to save us from inner attacks, then the outer attacks will diminish.

In our prayers, first we have to pray for the fulfilment of God's Will: "Let Thy Will be done." God's Fulfilment must be first and foremost. Then we can pray to God for special protection, so that when bad things occur, we will be somewhere else. If somebody hits my car from behind, we can say that an accident took place. But that very minute, with God's Grace, I could have been somewhere else – in another lane, or four cars ahead.

I tell my students to pray for a minute for protection before they start to drive. Previously, if they were in a car accident, they would say, "It was not my fault. Some other car hit me. I was innocent, helpless." But what good does this do? Today it is his fault; tomorrow it will be yours. What matters is not who is to blame, but how you can prevent the situation from occurring in the first place.

God will save us if our prayer is sincere. Unfortunately, instead of praying for inner wealth, which is illumination, we pray for material prosperity. But if we do not have inner prosperity, if we do not have peace, love and light, then even if we get outer prosperity, we will not have inner joy and security, for in the inner life we will be poverty-stricken. Similarly, if we pray to God for outer power, we may get it, but the more outer power we get, the more insecure we become.

Outer success is like a thick jungle. We may appreciate it, but there are quite a few tigers inside it. We cannot find any security there. Inner progress is like a garden with many beautiful and fragrant flowers. If we live in our heart-garden and feel our oneness with God and God's Compassion, then naturally we will be secure. Security is found only in our faith in God and in our realisation that we are of God and that God is of us.

God has asked a very simple question:
Do you want to be like Him?
He is eagerly waiting
For your open-hearted answer.

The All-Embracing Consciousness

When we feel our oneness with the rest of the world, then we never feel insecure. What is this feeling of universal oneness? It is the Consciousness of God, which is all-pervading and all-embracing.

An ordinary person may not think of God, but he immediately thinks of his brother, sister, friend, neighbour. But if he feels that the rest of the world is for him and that there is no difference between his existence and the existence of others, then his consciousness will immediately expand.

There is only one existence. The One has become many, like a tree with many branches and many leaves, many flowers and many fruits. In ordinary life, we immediately think of ourselves as individual entities. But if we can think of everyone as our very own, as part and parcel of our existence like the limbs of our body, then this problem of insecurity can be solved.

Insecurity goes away when we acquire the capacity of identification. Let us use the example of mothers and daughters. The mother is often jealous of her daughter because she is more beautiful or has a better education or job. The mother's jealousy takes the form of insecurity. She says, "Nobody appreciates me. Only my daughter is being appreciated." But if the mother is spiritual, she will immediately identify herself with her daughter's achievements and say, "I brought my daughter into the world and she is mine." A mother has every right to claim her daughter as her own. And when she claims and identifies herself with her daughter, if she feels that her daughter is but an extension of her own consciousness, there can be no insecurity.

Be not self-absorbed.
The world is a member
Of your immediate family.

Teamwork

During a shot-put competition, the spectators may see a person put the shot very far with his right hand. The right hand has thrown it, but immediately the left hand will feel that it also should get some credit. Even if someone says, "He has achieved the victory with his right hand," the left hand will not be jealous or insecure. The left hand did not throw the shot, true. But if that hand or any other part of the body had refused to co-operate, then there would have been no co-ordination of the body. When throwing the shot with the right hand, a counter-movement from the left hand and balance from the feet are necessary. When someone has stood first in shot-put, all parts of the body will feel that they have contributed by offering their capacity to bring about this achievement and success.

This principle applies in team sports also. If a team wins, the captain or leader often accepts the trophy, but the other players also get tremendous joy. They feel that it is their success, their achievement, for which he is receiving the award. In any activity, when the leader receives something, immediately the other members of the group should feel that it is their success, their combined achievement.

Whenever somebody else does something good, please feel that it is you who have done it. Do not think, "Oh, I have not done it. My name is not so-and-so." Your name is the Universal Consciousness. There is only one Being and that is the infinite and all-pervading "I". When any inhabitant of the universe achieves something, you can easily and most legitimately claim that you have achieved it, if you can just identify yourself with the Universal Consciousness.

Oneness is the perfect expansion
Of our inner reality.
Let our heart's oneness only increase
To make us feel
That we belong to a universal world-family,
And this world-family
Is a fulfilled Dream of God.

Guided By The Unseen Hand

We are bound to feel insecure as long as we do not feel the living Presence of God, as long as we feel that we are separated from God, our Source. If we can feel that God has sent us to earth to be His instruments, then we shall not feel insecure. If we can feel that our

Source is Light and Delight, and that at the end of our soul's journey, we shall return to that Source, then we will not feel insecure.

We can feel that our source is God only when we aspire, pray and meditate. When we do not, we are bound to feel that our source is something unknown and unknowable. To us this unknown and unknowable is ignorance. But the seeker who has set out on the spiritual path will feel that what is unknown today will become known tomorrow. Today his God is unknown but knowable. Tomorrow his God will be something known. The day after tomorrow his God will be at once the Knower and the Known.

You can easily become perfectly secure and fearless if you constantly think of yourself as God's chosen child, no matter what you do or how many deplorable mistakes you make in life. You have to feel that you are God's chosen instrument, and that you are eternally of Him and eternally for Him. You do not belong to anybody, you do not belong even to yourself; you belong only to Him, to the Supreme, to the Absolute Supreme in yourself. If you can feel this, then you are bound to feel perfectly secure and fearless.

When you feel that you are responsible, that you are doing and must do everything, then you are insecure. But if you feel that there is a higher force guiding your destiny, and that you are a mere instrument, then you will not feel insecure. To make the fastest progress, you have to cherish constant certainty that you are doing the right thing by God's infinite Grace. When you know who the Source is, you cannot be insecure.

Though I do not know
Where this next step leads,
I do know
An unseen Hand
Will guide me blessingfully
To my destination.

The Love Of The Gardener

If you say that you do not deserve God, who does? God-realisation is your birthright. From whom did you come? From God and nobody else. And where are you? In God. When you go back, where will you go? You will go back to God. We came from God, and we deserve Him because He is deep inside us and we have come here to express Him, to reveal Him.

The Creator has created your very existence. It is like the gardener who has created a garden with many beautiful flowers. If a flower says, "No, no, he does not love me, he does not love me!" is that not ridiculous? The very fact that the gardener has planted and cultivated the flowers – is this not his love? Every moment you have to feel that the Supreme does love you; otherwise, He would not have brought you into His world-creation. It is the Supreme who has created love.

If you can nourish and cherish the feeling that there is Someone who calls you His own, and that is God, the Inner Pilot, then your insecurity will vanish. Even in the ordinary world, when you know that a few friends or even one individual thinks of you and cares for you, you do not feel insecure. But now that you have entered into the spiritual life, you know that there is Someone who has infinite Power, who has infinite Patience, infinite Light, who cares for you and is more than eager to call you His very own.

You love God
Because He is Supreme.
God loves you
Because you are His Dream.
You need God
Because He is eternally perfect.
God needs you
Because you are His choice project.

The Reality Inside Us

You are the finite. If you want to become one with the Infinite, you have to surrender your existence to the Infinite. Offer your human life to the spiritual life, which is the Breath of the Divine. Always try to be aware of your Source, which is eternal peace, light and bliss. If your Source is something divine, eternal and infinite, then how can you feel insecure? If you can become consciously and constantly aware that you are of the Source and from the Source, if you can convince your mind that you came from light and delight and your ultimate Goal is to go back to light and delight, then you will have no sense of insecurity.

A person is insecure when he feels that darkness is all around him. If there is light all around us, we are not afraid. In the spiritual life we must always be aware of the fact that the Being who is inside us and around us is all light. And this Being is immortal. My hand is real, but it is not divinely real. It will die when I die. But my soul is divinely real, so it will remain eternally. The Reality inside us is divine and eternal. If we have something eternal within us to think of us and care for us, how can we feel insecure?

Never allow yourself to feel
That you are a failure.
God's Grace and God's Love
Will not approve of it.

The Most Secure Grasp

Insecurity comes only because your heart knows that your grasp on God is weak, and when temptation comes you will release Him and fall. But if you feel that God is holding you, then you will not feel

118

insecure, because you know that God has infinite strength to hold you fast inside His Heart.

Suppose you and God are together at a particular place and right in front of you is a deep hole. If you are holding your Father's hand, when temptation arises you may release your hold and try to grab that temptation. At that time, you will fall into the hole. But if you allow your Eternal Father to hold you, then even if temptation assails you, He will hold you so tightly that you will not be able to fall into the abyss of ignorance.

Once God clasps you, you cannot go away at all, and that is what you want. Since you have become spiritual, your goal is to be utilised by God according to His Will; you do not want to utilise God at your sweet will. You have to remain calm and quiet and let God clasp you and use you in His own Way.

If you have a true and sleepless
Love of God,
Then nobody will be able to snatch you away
From the embrace of God.

False Confidence And Real Confidence

Divine confidence says, "I can do this because something divine, God, is within me. That is why I can do this, why I can say this. But I could not do it otherwise. I can only mix with wisdom, light and delight because my Source is God. So I have confidence." It is like a child who knows that his parents are rich. He is confident because they have money. Here, our money is spiritual wealth. We feel that God, who is our Mother and Father, has infinite wealth, so we have confidence; we have peace of mind, light and bliss. Confidence we get when we see the Source within us, the Supreme.

119

Otherwise, in the ordinary life, there is no confidence at all. When we say that we have confidence, we know within ourselves that we are just showing off. We need confidence, but this is false confidence. It is something we have created in order to show off to the world and to other people.

When we are sincere, we immediately know that we are trying to fool others, but when we have divine confidence, we are not fooling anybody. We know that our Source is the Supreme, who has everything: infinite Peace, Light and Bliss. That is why we are confident. When we become one with Him, we know He will supply us with all His wealth in infinite measure. When we pray and meditate, we have that feeling. That is called real confidence; divine confidence.

> *God wants us to lose*
> *All our littleness*
> *So that He can bless us*
> *With His Eternity's Joy*
> *And*
> *His Infinity's Pride.*

Confidence Versus Ego

Ego wants to increase its power and lord it over others. Ego becomes powerful, more powerful, most powerful in order to dominate others. But self-confidence is a different matter. It comes from an inner source, a higher source. We get confidence from our inner existence, from our own inner reality. There is a divine root there. But ego does not have any root. Ego's root is only ignorance.

When we have the confidence to become good, we remember who we are: "I am God's child. I came here to work for God. I am not an unaspiring person. I am meant for the spiritual life. I have to realise God, because that is what God wants."

Ego does not care for God-realisation. In ego there is no sense of oneness; ego wants only to dominate others. Ego cares only for separation in order to show its existence. I, you, he, she – this is ego – whereas self-confidence will say, "I am all-pervading. If I am all-pervading, if I and my Father are one, then it is beneath my dignity to mix with anything that separates me from another creation of God." Self-confidence wants to become universal and shows its existence by becoming omnipresent, by becoming one with God.

My heart's constant guest:
God the Many.
My life's constant host:
God the One.

In The All-Loving Hands Of God

An unaspiring person is not sure of anything. He is at the mercy of all his whims. At this moment something may make him feel that he is absolutely useless and hopeless. At the next moment his ego will come forward and he will feel that he is everything, that he is the lord of the universe. Nothing is certain for the unaspiring person. But for an aspiring person, Eternity is certain because he knows and feels that he is in the flow of Eternity. He is the river which is entering into the ocean. He knows that inside him he has everything. Right now he is like a child. His Father cannot give him millions of dollars because, since he is only a child, he will misuse it. He knows that he can use only a dime or a quarter at this time, but he is certain that when he grows up, his Father will give him all His wealth: infinite Peace, Light and Bliss.

Our greatest protection lies not in our material achievements and resources. All the treasure of the world is emptiness to our divine soul. But if we can feel that there is Someone who thinks of us infinitely more than we think of ourselves, and if we can consciously say, "Eternal Father, Eternal Mother, You be responsible for what I do and say and grow into," then we will not worry about our destiny, for we will know and feel that it is in the all-loving Hands of God, who will do everything in us, through us and for us.

Let your heart
Tell your mind
That God is in full control
Of your life.
You will immediately see
That your tension has ceased
And your confidence
Has powerfully returned.

Fear

If you are brave enough
To sing through darkness,
Then light will sing through you
And for you.

Fear comes from darkness, from ignorance. If we enter into a room that is pitch dark, we will be frightened. But as soon as we turn on the light, the darkness is illumined and our fear vanishes. We see that there is nothing to fear in the darkness and that there is nothing to fear in the light either.

Fear is one of our most troublesome difficulties. Fear does not allow us to see the face of the ultimate Reality. It does not allow us to reach the Golden Shore of the Beyond. When we unconsciously cherish fear, it smilingly shakes hands with us. When we consciously think of fear, it triumphantly embraces us. But when we think of our inner courage, God cries with His divine Cry, for he feels that here He has a chosen instrument.

There is a well-known story about an old man walking along the street one evening who stepped on a rope. There was no light, and he thought the rope was actually a snake. Filled with fear, he let out a scream and ran away as fast as he could. While running he fell down and broke his leg. Some people nearby heard shouting and screaming, so they came with sticks. The old man was shouting all the time that there was a snake there. In the dark the others, too, thought it was a snake, so they started striking the rope and accidentally began hitting one another. The shouting and beating continued until another party

123

came with a light and discovered that it was just a piece of rope and not a snake.

When the light entered, the true reality was discovered. Similarly, in our human life, when light enters into our physical consciousness, every kind of fear is bound to disappear. But we are wanting in light, and that is why fear consciously and deliberately looms large in our life at every moment. But, if we are sincere enough to go deep within and to feel that inner courage belongs to us, then inner courage can dawn at every moment.

Failures: The Pillars Of Success

Why do we worry? We worry because we do not know what is going to happen to us tomorrow, or even in the next minute. We feel that if we do not do something for ourselves, then nobody is going to do it. But if we can feel that there is Someone who thinks of us infinitely more than we think of ourselves – our Inner Pilot – and if we can consciously offer our responsibility to Him, then our past, our present and our future become His problem. As very young children, we surrender to our parents and get, in return, protection. In our outer life we have become adults, but in the spiritual life we are still children, and at every moment we must try to listen to the dictates of our inner being.

Of course, we shall not commit any mistake consciously or deliberately. But if a mistake takes place in our inner nature, our vital, our physical or our mind, then immediately we should be ready to confess it without fear. What are mistakes, after all? The very idea of a mistake being shameful or unmentionable creates a wrong vibration in the cosmos. If we think a mistake is something that will inevitably be followed by punishment, then we are totally wrong.

First, let us take mistakes as failures. What are failures? They are the pillars of success. Failures are God's experiences in us, and He is carrying us towards the ultimate Goal, which is perfect Perfection. Second, let us take mistakes as half-truths. If we consider a mistake as an imperfect or an infinitesimal truth, if we can see in it an iota of truth, then we can feel that the mistake can be rectified or transformed into truth. What do we usually do? We separate ourselves from the mistake as if it were something dirty, ugly and obscene. Instead, let us take each mistake as a lump of clay that can be shaped and moulded into something useful.

Allow failure to teach you
A supreme lesson:
Each sunset is the beginning
Of a very, very bright
And powerful sunrise.

What Others Think

Why should you have to think of others or fear what they are thinking of you? If they feel that you are the worst person on earth, will it harm you? And if they think that you are the best person, will it bring your realisation of the Highest an inch closer?

You have to know who is dearest to you in this world. God is the dearest. You have to feel that if He is displeased with you, if He speaks ill of you, then you have to pay attention, because you do not want to hurt your dearest One. But if the world is displeased with you or speaks ill of you, then let the world play its role. If the world is going to bark, that does not mean you have to bark back. If you can see God as your only existence, then God will give you a sea of tranquillity, a sea of inner peace.

All the time you waste in thinking of what others are doing or what they are thinking of you could be used for your own self-discovery. If

125

you always think of God, God will think of you and appreciate you. In the outer life, when two people love each other, they are always thinking of each other and of what the other person is thinking of them. In the spiritual life also, cherish only these two thoughts: what God is thinking of you and what you are thinking of Him. Then there will be no time left for you to worry about what others are thinking of you. Let the whole world think ill of you; your God-realisation will not be delayed. Your realisation depends entirely upon your own aspiration.

Remember one thing,
Only one thing:
What others think of you
Will not and cannot change you,
Your capacity-world
And your quality-world.

Consciousness

One way to conquer fear is through the expansion of our consciousness. The creation around us is causing unnecessary fear in our mind or in our earthly existence precisely because we have not yet established our oneness-reality with it. If we pray and meditate soulfully, we establish a free access to the inner reality that pervades the entire outer world.

You are not afraid of your hand, your leg or your eye. Your consciousness pervades you from the soles of your feet to the crown of your head. You feel that these parts are yours, and that is why you are not afraid of them. But if you are afraid of someone who is beside, around or near you, it is because you have not enlarged your consciousness to include them.

You are not afraid of your limbs because they are yours. You claim them as your very own. But when you go beyond your own boundaries and do not enlarge or expand your consciousness, you feel alienated; you feel everybody is a stranger to you. When we practise yoga, the union of the individual soul with the Supreme Self, we try to enlarge our consciousness until the time comes when it pervades the length and breadth of the world. With our conscious awareness we become one, totally one, with the universe. Then there can be no fear.

Fear exists just because we want to remain separated, consciously or unconsciously, from the all-pervading Reality that we eternally are. For a seeker, the paramount thing is to dive deep within and discover the road that leads to this all-pervading oneness-reality. Where there is oneness, inseparable oneness, there cannot be even an iota of fear.

The mind creates division,
And division is another name
For devastating pain.
The heart creates oneness,
And oneness is another name
For spontaneous joy.

Acceptance Of The Infinite

So long as there is even an iota of fear in you, the undivine forces have the power to attack you mercilessly. But if you do not have fear and if you are sure of your goal, then the undivine forces can never attack. If you can accept Infinity as something which is your own but which you have forgotten about, if you can see that you have always been that Infinity, then fear does not come.

Sometimes you are afraid of the Infinite that your highest part wants to enter into fully. On the one hand, you want to dive into the sea of Infinity. On the other hand, you have a feeling of uncertainty. You wonder what you are going to get from the sea of Infinity. You have to know that you are going to get the infinite wealth of the immortal Consciousness that pervades the entire universe. Your soul wants it, but your mind is afraid.

Try, if you can, to empty your mind daily. The mind is full of doubt, obscurity, ignorance, suspicion and so forth. Early in the morning you can try, say for ten minutes, to conquer thought – not to allow any thought to enter, good, bad, divine or undivine. Feel that your mind is like a vessel. First you empty it. Now you are waiting – for what? For peace, light and bliss. Allow only the divine thoughts that are your friends.

In the beginning you do not know who your friends are and who your enemies are. You have to be very careful. Later on you allow only your friends, that is to say, divine thoughts, progressive thoughts, illumined thoughts. These thoughts will undoubtedly conquer fear in the mind on your behalf.

> *As long as you are willing*
> *To muster your inner courage*
> *To achieve a perfect life,*
> *God's Compassion-Flood*
> *Will, without fail,*
> *Wait for you.*

The Spiritual Light

Inside you is God and the effulgence of divine light. You want to see light. Either you are trying to enter into the vastness of this light, or you are trying to bring to the fore the light that you already have. But there are many people who are afraid of light. They say, "Yes, we want light," but the moment it comes to them, they feel that they are going to be caught. People feel that if they can hide themselves in a dark room, then they will be in a position to see the world and pass judgement, but that nobody will be able to see them. Their darkness, they feel, is a kind of safety and security. When light comes and is ready to enter into them, they feel that all their weaknesses and limitations, all their negative ideas and thoughts, will be exposed.

Many people do not go to spiritual Masters for this reason. Why? They feel that spiritual Masters will immediately see through them and say, "Oh, you did such bad things just yesterday or a few months ago!" People do not want to be exposed to the light, although we all need light. But this attitude is a deplorable mistake. The spiritual light will never expose anything. On the contrary, it will illumine and transform them.

When a mother notices the shortcomings, imperfections and weaknesses of her child, what does she do? She hides them carefully and secretly. She will never even imagine exposing her own child to the world. In the spiritual life, the seeker has to feel that he is a child of the Divine Mother. She is infinitely more loving and compassionate then the human mother, so how can She expose Her child? She only hides his teeming imperfections and secretly makes him aware of his shortcomings. She does this precisely because She does not want him to always repeat the same mistakes. But She does not stop here. She carries the child one step forward and transforms his life of night into a life of light.

Your physical being may be afraid of the dark night of the past, but you must always look forward, look ahead. The past is dust. If the past comes and tortures your mind with what you did two weeks ago or two hours ago, and if this past is not inspiring or encouraging, throw it into the dust again. The past is to be buried. Your spiritual existence has to grow from where you now stand.

If you can obliterate the past and be ready to enter into the ever-new, consciously and soulfully, you will see that the new also has its reality, a more fulfilling reality than the past. Then there can be no fear, never. Fear comes only when either you are unwilling to give up your old life or you are not certain of the new life. But if you cry for light, light will guide you because that is its very nature. The purpose of your life is to become the light itself. If you wholeheartedly and spontaneously cry for light, then there can be no fear.

> *Go forward!*
> *Dive inward!*
> *Fly upward!*
> *Daring is the best form*
> *Of loving God.*

Many Ways To The Goal

The heart of spirituality is yoga, or conscious oneness with God. Religion is a house, and yoga is a path that leads to God. Each of us has to remain in our own house, but we have every right to walk along the same road to go to school and get knowledge. The road belongs to everyone.

Some people are afraid of practising meditation just because meditation is new to them. Anything that is new to us often creates fear in us. In some religious traditions, prayer has been given much more importance than meditation. People feel that if they meditate instead of praying, then they are being disloyal to their religious beliefs. You do not have to give up your religion in order to practise meditation.

The very purpose of meditation is to unite, expand, enlighten and immortalise our consciousness. When we meditate, we enter into our own Divinity, which has infinite Power. When we have free access to Divinity, when our entire existence, inner and outer, is surcharged with Divinity's boundless and infinite Power, then how can we be afraid? It is impossible!

A true seeker is he
Who is always eager
To come and play
In the Supreme's Heart-Garden
Of Ecstasy.

God The Love

If you are going to your father's house, naturally it is easy to get in; the door is always open to you. It is extremely easy to visit God if you realise that you belong to God and that He is yours to visit. But it is extremely difficult to visit God if you think of Him as a foreigner, as someone unrelated to you. In that case, the door is shut and it is extremely difficult to open it.

The greatest obstacle in our contact with God is fear. Our conception of God is so peculiar. We feel that He is like a primary school teacher who is ready to beat us black and blue if we deviate an inch from the path of Truth. But that conception of God is absurd. There is only one God, and that is God the Love.

To approach God with fear or through fear is very unhealthy. We must not fear God's Justice and we must not fear God. If we fear God, we will never be able reach Him, we will never be able to get anything from Him. The moment we are afraid of someone, his reality and our reality become separate. If a child is afraid of his father, he will not be able to receive anything from him – he will not even go to him.

Fear is one thing; reverential awe is something else. Reverential awe is the feeling that someone is a little higher than you, so you have to behave well. God is infinitely better than you in every way, so you feel that you must have that kind of reverence. Deeper than reverence is love, true love. A child does not need reverence; he does not have

131

to show reverence because he knows he has love, which is infinitely more effective. A child does not have to go and touch his father's feet at every second. The moment he shows his father his love, his heart, that is enough.

We feel that what our father has, we also have. Unfortunately, we are still children; that is why our father is unable to give his vast wealth to us. But when the child grows up, he gets what his father has and what his father is. If we can love God soulfully, then God will give us everything.

When a child is playing in the mud and then all of a sudden he is called by his mother, he is not afraid that she will beat him because he is dirty. He will go running to her, and she will immediately take his dirt, his filth, as her very own. She will wash him in order to show others that her son is also very clean. We have to approach God like that. No matter how many undivine things we do, we run towards Him and feel that with His Compassion He will just clean us immediately.

Slowly and steadily
God is bringing to the fore
My God-love-capacity
From my heart's deepest chamber.

Conquering The Fear Of Death

You can think of death in a way that is most significant and, at the same time, most reassuring. In your house you have quite a few rooms. One room you use as your living room, another as your office and another as your bedroom. During the course of the day you do many things. For a few hours you work in your office, for a few hours you are in your living room and for a few hours you are in your bedroom sleeping. You cannot do any one thing for twenty-four hours a day. You cannot work for twenty-four hours a day because your body needs rest. Again, you cannot sleep for twenty-four hours a day. You divide your time.

Each room has a significant role to play. You are not afraid of any of these rooms. When you go to sleep, you do not say, "I have no idea if I will ever wake up tomorrow!" No, when you are tired, you go to your bedroom, and the next morning when your body is refreshed, you wake up. Similarly, in your existence-house you have one room called death and one room called life. When you become tired and want to take rest, you will go to your other room. You have to feel that both rooms belong to you and are part and parcel of your existence.

Right now you are afraid of death because you think of yourself as your body, your mind, your senses. But a day will come when, on the strength of your aspiration, prayer and meditation, you will think of yourself not as the body but as the soul. You will think of yourself as a conscious instrument of God. Since God is omnipresent, and He is utilising you to manifest Himself, how can He ever abandon you to death?

Conquering the fear of death depends on how much love you have for God and how sincerely you need Him. If your need for God is soulful, devoted and constant, then in the inner world you establish a free access to God's Love, Compassion and Concern. Then how can you be afraid of death? The moment you feel that you need God and He needs you, the moment you feel God inside you, before you and around you, then death no longer exists for you. This physical body may leave the earth, but the soul, which is a conscious portion of God, will remain consciously in God and for God throughout Eternity.

It is up to you to think of yourself as the body or as the soul. If you think of yourself as the soul, that means you have already developed an inner connection with God. If you know that the soul is your real reality, you will not have any fear of death.

My Lord Supreme,
Do widen the narrow rivulet
Of my life
So that I can forever surely flow
Into Your Heart's Ecstasy-Ocean.

The Rising Flame

Our body is limited; that is why the body has fear. Our vital is unconscious; that is why the vital has fear. Our mind is obscure; that is why the mind has fear. Our heart is unaspiring; that is why the heart has fear.

To free our body from fear, what we need is the glorious experience of our soul. To free our vital from fear, what we need is the dynamic and conscious expansion of our soul. To free our mind from fear, what we need is the transforming illumination of our soul. Finally, to free our heart from fear, what we need is the fulfilling perfection of our soul.

Fear will leave us when we feel that we are destined to do something for God. The word "destined" brings boundless courage to the fore. Even if somebody is weak by nature, if someone says that he is destined to work for God, then immediately from the inner world heroism comes forward. He will fight against any obstruction with a strength and inner determination that will surprise him. Obstructions may come in the form of impurity, obscurity, jealousy, fear and doubt, but the word "destined" will smash the pride of all the negative forces. Anything that is undivine will have to surrender to the power of this word.

There can be no fear when we live in the effulgence of the soul. To live constantly in the divine effulgence of our soul, only one thing is needed: a conscious inner cry. When this mounting flame within us rises up towards the Highest, it illumines everything around it. Darkness is transformed into light, doubt into certainty, fear into strength and death into Immortality.

Since your heart was awakened,
You have been praying and meditating
To see divine light.
And this light itself wants you to see
That there is another world
Where truth, peace and bliss abide.

Doubt

Do not doubt
The existence of Truth
If you cannot see the Truth.

In the spiritual life we constantly fight. We do not fight against an enemy outside ourselves, but we fight against our own inner enemies: fear, doubt, anxiety and worry. In comparison with doubt, all other obstacles pale into insignificance. If a seeker is making very fast progress or when he has gone a long way in the spiritual life, even then he may be a victim of doubt. I always say that doubt is slow poison.

You are God's chosen child. When you go deep within and accept the spiritual life, you have to feel that doubt is the worst thief in your life. It is taking away all your precious inner wealth. Also, doubt is your worst enemy. Why? Because doubt starts doubting itself. Today you doubt someone and tomorrow you doubt yourself. Today you have come to one conclusion and tomorrow another wave of doubt envelops you. But that does not mean that today's doubt is washed away. No, it has only been replaced by another doubt.

In life, everything depends on love. Unfortunately, some people love doubt. Outwardly they say they hate it, but inwardly, unconsciously or consciously, they cherish it. They feel that if they do not doubt, they are not wise. When the mind doubts someone, it feels great satisfaction in becoming the judge. The moment we doubt someone, we feel that we are a step higher than they are. This is absolutely wrong. In the spiritual life nobody is superior and nobody is inferior. We are all instruments manifesting different aspects of God's multiplicity.

Beyond Reason Is Truth

When doubt assails you, it will try to make you feel that it is good to doubt. It will say, "Doubt as much as you can. Only then can you discover the reality." Doubt will send its best friend, the reasoning mind, to live with you. The reasoning mind will come and tell you that it can offer you the greatest satisfaction and fulfilment. But in the spiritual life the reasoning mind is useless and doubt is worse than useless.

Intellectual life is good and helpful before you have entered into spirituality. But once you have started concentrating and meditating and getting inner experiences on the strength of your inner and higher aspiration, you must not accept the feast of reason.

In the beginning many things help us, but later they may become obstacles. Desire was a help when it raised us out of the world of lethargy, but it becomes a hindrance when we want to enter into the world of spirituality. Once we have some mental capacity, we must begin to transcend our servitude to the mind by bringing down the Grace, from Above to illumine the mind. We have to go farther, deeper and higher than the world of reason, far beyond the reasoning or intellectual mind. The reasoning mind has to be transformed into a dedicated instrument of the Supreme.

If we live in the mind, we will constantly try to circumscribe the Truth; we will never be able to see the Truth in its proper form. Only if we live in the soul will we be able to embrace the Truth as a whole. Beyond reason is Truth. Reason has very limited light, whereas what we want and need has infinite Light. When infinite Light dawns, reason is broken into pieces.

> My Supreme,
> A man-made volcano-mind
> I was,

137

But now I am a God-made
Heart-fountain.

The Questioning Mind And The Searching Mind

It is not at all necessary to understand something intellectually. There have been many spiritual giants who did not use the mind; they used the heart instead. Right now we have the feeling that the answer of the intellect is as adequate as the answer of the heart. But a day will come when we will feel that it is only the heart that can give us the real answer.

The intellect is very limited, but the soul is unlimited. For this reason an aspirant dives deep into the inmost recesses of his heart, for it is there that the soul abides. The Truth can be known only through aspiration. The true attributes of God are Peace, Light, Bliss and Power. These attributes all exist in boundless measure in the heart of Eternity. Only the seeker of Truth who aspires to go beyond the domain of the intellect can enter into the Light, Peace, Bliss and Power of the highest Absolute. Not intellect but psychic aspiration is needed to know and to realise the attributes of God.

You may say, "I question because I do not understand. I want to understand." But "understanding" is a very tricky word. When today we understand something in a particular way, that very understanding may not satisfy us tomorrow. We may develop another kind of understanding and see that yesterday's understanding was absolutely useless.

You have to know that the questioning mind is the precursor of the doubting mind. You do not stop with the questioning mind. Today you question someone, tomorrow you doubt him. Again, just because you doubt, you question. It is better not to have a questioning mind. You can have a searching mind. With the searching mind, you are searching for the Reality. That is good. But in the other case, either the questioning mind is the harbinger of the doubting mind or they are most intimate friends.

> *Do anything in your power*
> *To prevent self-doubt*
> *From torturing you.*

Silence Liberates

Again, we cannot say that God does not exist in the intellect. God is omnipresent. But if one wants to know God's highest Height, His deepest Depth, His all-pervading Consciousness, then one can never know these through the intellect. We can best silence the sounds of our mind by knowing that whatever the mind gives is insufficient. It will never be able to give us a sense of satisfaction and perfection. But what will the heart give us? The heart will give us the message of inseparable oneness with the Absolute, the Highest, the Universal and the Transcendental.

A seeker has to know the limitations of the mind. But the heart only wants to melt into the infinite Vast. A drop wants to enter into the mighty ocean and cries to become the ocean itself. If we have that kind of inner awareness, then we will be able to silence our mind and expand our heart.

There lived a pious man in Bengal, India. Every day a Sanskrit scholar would come to his house and read aloud a few soul-stirring spiritual teachings from the Gita, the Upanishads and the Vedas. The master of the house was an aspirant. He would listen most devotedly to these discourses.

The family had a bird called Krishna. Krishna was kept in a cage in the room where the discourses were given. It also listened to these talks. One day the bird spoke to its master, "Could you please tell me what benefit you actually derive from these spiritual talks?"

The master answered, "O Krishna, you do not seem to understand that these spiritual talks will liberate me, free me from bondage!"

The bird said, "You have been listening to these discourses for the last few years, but I do not see any change in you. Would you kindly ask your teacher what will happen to you?"

On the following day the master of the house said to his teacher, "Guru, I have been listening to your spiritual talks for the last ten years. Is it not true that I will get liberation and freedom?"

The teacher kept quiet. He scratched his head, pondered over the question, but found no reply. He just remained unhappily silent for about an hour and then left the house.

The master of the house was stunned. His Guru could not give an answer to the bird's question, but the bird found an answer.

From that day on, the bird stopped eating. It stopped even its usual chirping. It became absolutely silent. The master and his family placed food inside the cage every day, but the bird would not touch anything. One day the master looked at the bird and, seeing no sign of life in it, took it gently out of the cage. With a tearful heart, he placed his Krishna on the floor. In a twinkling, the bird flew away into the infinite freedom of the sky!

The bird taught. Its master and his Guru learned: silence liberates.

If you like the heart's way,
Then the distance
From captivity to liberation
Is quite short.

Doubt Versus Trust

If you have a sincere question, there is only one place to go to get the best possible answer and that is the soul. The soul will answer you through the heart. Otherwise, no matter what kind of answer you get, your mind will doubt it. It will contradict all suggestions and advice, and then a few seconds later it will doubt its own discovery. The decisions of the mind are constantly changing, so you can never find real certainty and satisfaction on the path of the mind. But when the heart gives you an answer, it is a permanent reality. If you follow the path of the heart, you see that it immediately identifies with the reality – no matter what the substance or essence of the reality is. Then, once the heart brings you the answer, you bring it into the intellect.

If you want to know if something is true without using the mind, then meditate on it. When you use the intellectual mind, constantly you are scrutinising things, but you are never satisfied. The intellect is like a sharp knife that is constantly trying to see what is in something. It cuts the thing into tiny pieces and then tries to see what is inside each piece. It tries to see the reality in its smallest form. When we stay in the soul, Truth's very existence is its own proof. When we come into the world, our very first step is belief. When you say to your child, "This is fire, this is a knife. Do not touch them because they will hurt you," the child believes you. He has no need to ask for proof.

> O seeker, just try to offer
> Your tender trust.
> Yours will be, before long,
> The thunder-victory.

Doubting Ourselves Or Loving Ourselves

We should ask ourselves whether we accomplish anything by doubting others. If we doubt somebody's achievement to the very end of our days, our doubt will not take away from his achievement. If he has achieved something, it is done and our doubt cannot diminish it.

But if we start doubting ourselves, that is our real destruction. The moment we start doubting our own possibilities, potentialities and capabilities, we can no longer progress.

If you now doubt me and feel that I am not a sincere seeker, a few moments later you will feel that I am sincere, and a few moments later you will doubt your own capacity to judge. Now, when you doubted me, I did not lose anything, and when you had faith in me, you did not lose anything. But when you started doubting your own judgement, then you lost everything.

The greatest obstacle on the spiritual path is self-doubt. If you doubt God, that is one thing. There is no harm in it. God will not lose any of His infinite capacities because of your doubt. But if you start doubting yourself, then you are totally lost. All of your inner capacities will be washed away in the torrent of your self-doubt.

You should not doubt God and you should not doubt yourself. But if you have to doubt one of the two, then the best thing is to doubt God. God's existence you can doubt if you want to because He is not standing right in front of you; you do not see Him or consciously feel Him. Each time a doubt comes and we feel that we are not God's instrument, we fall short of our capacity. How many times we doubt ourselves, belittle ourselves. The moment we doubt that God is inside us, a dark spot appears on the golden tablet of our heart. When we do not love ourselves, the face of the sun is covered with clouds. The moment we belittle our capacity and doubt ourselves, the moment we forget what we eternally are, at that time we are millions of miles from the truth. We love ourselves only when we feel that we have achieved something or feel that tomorrow or the day after we are going to do something. This is the human in us.

Who is God? God is our highest part, our most illumined part. When we as individuals enter into our highest consciousness and know that we are in all, of all and for all, at that time we do not doubt ourselves. At that time, we are everything, so who can doubt whom?

We embody God and want to reveal and manifest God, so we do not even dream of minimising our capacity. Here we are spontaneously embodying and revealing the divine. When the real, the highest, the most illumined part in us comes to the fore, at that time we really love ourselves because we know who we are.

Who am I?
A beautiful love-beam
From God's Heaven.
What shall I become?
A perfection-dream
For the world's soul.

Moving Beyond Doubt

Sometimes when you have doubt, you cherish it, while at the same time wishing that this doubt could be conquered. When I say that you cherish something, I mean that you get a kind of subtle joy from it. When doubt first starts, it is like a tiny child. When a little child pinches an adult, just because it is such a little child, the adult does not stop him. He feels pain, but also he gets a kind of joy that such a tiny little thing is pinching him. Then, as the child gets older, the adult lets the child keep on pinching him. But when the child becomes an adolescent, when he pinches the adult, it will really hurt. Finally, when he grows up, he will really give the adult a blow.

When doubt starts out, it is tiny. It gives you a little pain, but also it gives you a little joy. You feel that you are protecting it, that you are in control. You feel that you can throw it out at any time. You allow an undivine thought, or doubt, to come into your house. But once it enters, it grows. When you cherish it, it feels that the house is really its own. Then it is in charge of you.

143

Some people feel that if today they cherish doubts, tomorrow they will be able to conquer them at their sweet will. But tomorrow will never come in their lives. Their nature's transformation will never take place so long as they cherish that kind of idea. If you do not begin immediately, you will never begin.

You may say, "Previously I had more doubt than now, so I am gradually making progress." But it is not useful to compare yourself with your obscure past. You should compare yourself with your golden future. Feel that you have to fight until the end. Today you may feel that you have conquered a little, but a few days later you will see that, like a wave, all these wrong forces have entered into your consciousness again and you are back where you started. Whenever you are aware of any wrong movement within you, immediately overcome it, like a divine hero.

Again, some aspirants have the complacent feeling that they have walked a long distance and now they can take rest. But this is also a serious mistake. Even if you have only one more step to go in order to reach the ultimate Goal, you must not take rest. Even on the verge of realisation many spiritual seekers have fallen. They have been swept away by temptation or doubt, and only after many, many years have they been able to resume their spiritual life again. So you have to always be on the alert. You have to move forward continually.

Life,
Like a river,
Always wants to go forward.

The Light Of The Soul

When doubt enters into you, you can take it as a monkey that is constantly bothering you. You are praying and meditating, but you let the monkey go on and on because you are patient. There is a competition between your patience and the monkey's mischievous pranks. Just because you are a seeker, you are bound to have more patience than someone who is not aspiring, so the monkey's patience can never equal yours. If you are not paying attention to it, the monkey will eventually feel that it is beneath its dignity to bother you again and again. Patience has such capacity to dissolve wrong forces. If you have the capacity to ignore or constantly reject the negative forces, they can never win.

There is another way. If doubt enters, you have to think of the antidote for doubt, which is faith. If doubt is entering into your mind, immediately utter the word "faith" and have faith in yourself. We can conquer doubt just by meditating on the soul or thinking always of the soul. If we identify ourselves with the mind, we will not have the power to conquer all doubt, because the mind itself unconsciously or consciously cherishes doubt. We should try to save ourselves with the light of the soul. Every day, before doubt has the opportunity to enter into our mind, we should try to feel the light of the soul inside us.

The soul is infinitely more powerful than our mental doubt. We can and we should take the positive side. We came from the soul. Inside us is the soul; we are the soul and we are for the soul. Always we can try to identify our physical being with the soul, which is all light and delight. When we feel at every moment that we are growing into the soul's light and delight, then doubt can easily be transformed into divine confidence. At that time we will say, "I am God's child. If I cannot do it, who can? I can and I shall realise God, I can and I must manifest God." We can cherish that kind of divine awareness. Then doubt is bound to leave us.

When I am in the soul
And for the soul,

God gives me the capacity
To see the panorama
Of His universal Game.

Doubt-Clouds, Aspiration-Sun

Before the day dawns, darkness is our teacher. At that time there is no hope. Then, when the sun comes, darkness is gone. But again, during the day many times we notice clouds obscuring the sky. Like that, in the spiritual life doubt comes and disappears. When it disappears, at that time the eternal sun shines most powerfully within us.

It is your soul that represents the natural state of consciousness. But doubt makes it difficult to realise the soul. Doubt is the seeker's fruitless struggle in the outer world. Aspiration is the seeker's fruitful confidence in the inner world. Doubt struggles and struggles. Finally it defeats its own purpose. Aspiration flies upward to the Highest. At its journey's end it reaches the Goal. Doubt is based on outer observation. Aspiration is founded on inner experience. Doubt ends in failure because it lives in the finite physical world. Aspiration ends in success because it lives in the ever-climbing soul.

Doubt will never tell us the truth about where we stand or what we stand for. When we spontaneously, consciously, deliberately and soul-fully cast aside doubt from our existence, God-realisation becomes easy. And how can we cast aside this doubt, this slow poison, from our existence? We can do so only on the strength of our constant aspiration, flowing determination, total self-giving and love, devotion and surrender.

My all-powerful Lord
Tells my soulful heart
That my ferociously doubtful mind
Is nothing but a paper tiger.

Lethargy

How can you reach the land of peace
When you cling to your old
Lethargy-armchair
And do not even want
To stand up and move?

There are many people who say, "O God, I am in Your eternal time. I will lead an ordinary life. You give me illumination in Your own time." But this is the wrong attitude. When depression, frustration, worry and anxiety come and attack us and make us feel that we will never realise God, that time is very short, then we have to take shelter in Eternity. But this feeling of Eternity should not make us say, "Oh, we can wallow in the pleasures of idleness because we are eternal and, of course, one day we will realise God." We must try our utmost to realise God here and now, at this very moment, while at the same time offering ourselves devotedly and soulfully at the Feet of the Supreme.

In the spiritual life, the awakening of the soul is not enough. Many people are awakened to the truth, to the inner life. But after being awakened, one has to dive, one has to run, one has to fly. One has to dive into the innermost, run to the farthest, fly to the highest. Only then can the seeker's awakening blossom into the flower of realisation.

For a spiritual person, Eternity is nothing but the eternal Now. We have to work very hard every second for our illumination – through our dedicated service, through our prayer, through our meditation. Then, after we have done our part, we surrender to God's Will. At that time we will see that our realisation does not depend on our personal effort; it depends entirely on God's Grace. Even our personal effort depends on God's Grace. But God will give us His Grace only when He feels that we have played our role. When we have played our role, then He will play His role.

With our own determination
And with Grace from Above
We will be able to succeed
Without fail
And to proceed
In an amazing way!

The Satisfaction Of The True Aspirant

There are two types of satisfaction. One type of satisfaction we see in the laziest person. This type of person has no desire, nothing. He does not want to make any progress. He is in the world of ignorance. On the physical plane, a lazy person's satisfaction means that he does not have to work; he does not even have to climb down the staircase. He has stayed in bed five hours after the sun has risen, so he is satisfied because he did not have to budge an inch. But although he is satisfied on the physical plane, on the mental plane, undivine thoughts are making a big hole in his mind.

A lazy person can never be divinely satisfied even for one minute. True, there are people who do not work, yet appear to be satisfied, but they are actually not. Their satisfaction with doing nothing is no satisfaction; it is stagnation. But there is another type of satisfaction. This type comes when we are praying, concentrating, meditating, doing our best, feeling that God is our all-loving Father, and knowing that He will give us what we actually need at His choice Hour.

One who is divinely satisfied says, "God knows what is best for me. He has given me what I actually need. I am praying, I am concentrating, I am meditating, and He is helping me. I am happy with Him. I know it is His business to give me full realisation, infinite Light, at His choice Hour. At the same time I am trying my utmost to realise God. I am making this personal effort with my utmost love, devotion and aspiration. I am satisfied with what I am and what I have." This is the satisfaction of the true aspirant who does not demand anything from God.

If you really want to have
A satisfaction-day,
Then immediately cancel your friendship
With lethargy-night.

Positive Prayer

Swami Vivekananda was a great spiritual figure who lived about a century ago. He once said to his disciples, "You are lazy people! You will realise God sooner if you play football instead of reading the Bhagavad Gita. Go and play football!" His disciples were so lethargic. They were talking and talking about God, but they were doing nothing. They did not want to move an inch.

We have to be active and dynamic inwardly as well as outwardly. All of us have prayed to God to fulfil certain desires. Is it not a crime to ask for good things: "God, give me peace, give me joy, give me love." Then you can say, "God, it is up to You whether to give me these things today or tomorrow, in ten days' time or in twenty years' time." God will be happy that you are asking Him for peace. Then a day will come when you will have peace, love and light in a very large measure. At that time you can start telling God, "Give me whatever You want to give me. Do whatever You want to do with my life."

It is on the strength of your prayer and meditation that you will be able to become one with God's Will. If you do not pray or meditate, you will simply be lethargic. You will wallow in the pleasures of idleness and say, "Oh, God will do everything for me." Why should God do anything for lazy seekers? You have to make a choice whether you want light or darkness.

God compassionately asks me,
"Will you be available?"
He never asks me,
"Will you be able?"

Meditation Is A Golden Opportunity

Each moment is an opportunity. Each moment during meditation is the greatest opportunity, no matter what consciousness you were in the rest of the day, or even just before you sat down to meditate. During each moment of meditation, the Supreme is knocking at your heart's door. He stands before your heart's door and knocks for you to open it. If you keep it closed, He just goes away. God has good manners. He does not want to be an intruder.

Once you have accepted the spiritual life, you have to be extremely wise. Each moment during meditation is a golden opportunity. Each moment is important in your life, but each second during meditation is of utmost importance. During meditation you can throw any undivine thoughts or ideas into the ocean of the Supreme's Compassion.

Sometimes after meditating for half an hour, people feel that they can relax for hours because they have played their role. But your inner cry must be constant and dynamic. Then gradually you will get inner peace in the body, in the vital, in the mind and in the heart.

In the beginning you have to work hard. You have to struggle in order to cry constantly. But once you are in motion, there is no worry. When you want to drive a car, you have to turn the key and do various other things. But when the engine is running, at that time you can relax. Similarly, in meditation you need the dynamic inner cry first. Only then can you get the divine peace and poise. Real spiritual poise is not a matter of self-deception. Pay all attention to your dynamic inner cry. It will lead you to the Goal.

A new creation
Can dawn in you
When your mind is
Totally empty of thoughts
During your meditation.

Self-Control In The Conscious Mind

The Supreme empties our inner receptivity-vessel at night so that we can fill ourselves with His divine Light in the morning. That is the spiritual reason for sleep, and that is why we should always meditate early in the morning before we begin our daily activities. However, if you sleep more than your body's necessity, then a disproportionate amount of lethargy attacks your body. Because of this merciless attack, you feel more tired, so you should try to know whether your body really needs more sleep or whether it is only your mind which is making you feel tired.

What you can do if you feel that even eight hours of sleep is not enough for you, or if you are unable to get to bed at your usual hour on a certain night, is this: try to imagine that you are going to sleep

151

for twenty-four hours. Then as soon as you wake up in the morning, try to feel that you have slept for twenty-four hours. Never think that you have slept for only three hours or four hours. It is the mind that convinces the outer consciousness. If your conscious mind tells you that you have slept for twenty-four hours, then you will believe it. This is not self-deception. It is self-control in the conscious mind. We say that we have slept for twenty-four hours because this figure has enormous strength. We may not sleep for even four hours, but the figure twenty-four immediately gives us a sense of satisfaction, relief and fulfilment. In this way we can get up early in the morning.

There is also a yogic method of getting rest. In one second you can take the rest of fifteen minutes, half an hour or even more. How can you get that kind of rest? When you go to sleep at night, feel that your whole body from head to foot has become a sea of peace. You have become peace itself. Consciously try to feel that you are not the body, but an infinite expanse of peace. When you can consciously feel this peace, you will see that your physical body has merged with it and totally disappeared in the sea of peace. If you can do this exercise effectively, you will need very little sleep.

It is not the number of hours you sleep that is important. During eight hours of sleep you may not get even one hour of sound sleep, and perhaps you will not even get a couple of minutes. If you take coffee ten times a day, then bring it down to nine times, eight times, seven times and so on. In exactly the same way, you can try to reduce the amount you sleep. If you want to suddenly bring it down from seven hours to four hours, you may perhaps do it for two days. Then, on the third day, you will not be able to get up. You will say, "I have meditated for so many days. Let me take rest." Everything has to be done very, very slowly, regularly and systematically. If you have been accustomed to sleeping for seven hours, then please try to sleep only fifteen minutes less. Try to continue with six hours and forty-five minutes for a few weeks or a few months. In this way it will be possible for you to sleep less. There is no shortcut. If you try to bring it down from seven hours to four or three, it will tell upon your health. But if you do it slowly, regularly and systematically, it is not only quite possible but inevitable.

If you meditate and concentrate, what is necessary is to feel the infinite expanse of peace and to embody peace inside you. We feel that when the body is active and dynamic, we have strength. But the real strength is in inner peace, not outer action. When we have peace in infinite measure, then automatically dynamic energy comes from there. In the outer field of manifestation we become dynamic energy, while inside we are all peace.

> *This is my day:*
> *I love it.*
> *This is my morning God-Hour:*
> *I need it.*
> *This is my supreme moment:*
> *I am it.*

Creating Energy

Another spiritual method that can come to your rescue when you are tired is to do alternate breathing exercises for a few minutes.

Start by using your right thumb to close your right nostril. Next you breathe in with the left nostril, silently repeating the name of God, just once. Then close the left nostril with the fourth finger of the right hand, and with both nostrils closed, silently repeat the name of God, four times while holding the breath. Finally you lift the thumb from the right nostril, still keeping the left nostril closed, and exhale, repeating the name of God, twice. After some time you can gradually increase the number. Instead of this short one-four-two breath, you can practise a four-sixteen-eight count breath, but it should be done comfortably without strain.

If you can practise this exercise, the benefits will be unimaginable. But do not do it mechanically. Concentrate while you are breathing, and you are bound to feel that you are breathing in divine energy.

Another way to overcome lethargy is by repeating "Supreme" as fast as possible. You do not have to shout at the top of your lungs, but you have to be able to hear it; do not do it in silence. You can be seated in your room or walking in a silent place where nobody is going to hear you, but you should not do it while lying down.

While you are chanting "Supreme", imagine everything that is inside you, starting with your toes. Think of your muscles, nerves, blood or anything that you want, and try to feel that the Supreme is entering into that particular part of your body. Then move to other parts of your body. You do not have to see what is inside your legs or your heart or your brain. Only imagine that something is there, and that that very thing is being touched by the word "Supreme". If lethargy has already stationed itself inside your knee or shoulder or somewhere else, that portion of the being has to be touched by the very presence of the Supreme. Each time you say "Supreme", chanting as fast as possible, try to feel that the Power of the Supreme, the Life of the Supreme and the Divinity of the Supreme are entering into you.

You can become dynamic also by repeating the word "dynamism". The word dynamism has tremendous power. As soon as you utter the word "dynamism," you are bound to feel tremendous strength, either in your arms, your legs, your head or your heart. Each time you repeat the word "dynamism", a portion of your body will be surcharged with dynamism. Although right now only a portion of you responds to the word dynamism, when you repeat the word, there will come a time when, from the soles of your feet to the top of your head, dynamism will flow.

Do not just sit there.
Stand up!
Do not just stand.
Start running!
If you cannot run,
Start walking at least.
Can you not see that your Beloved Supreme
Is eagerly waiting for you?

The Goal Is Within Reach

In order to have constant dynamism, you have to be constantly aware of your Goal and you have to feel that it is very close. It is not millions of miles away; it is around you, before you, in front of your nose. You have only to seek it consciously, grasp it and claim it. You have to always have the feeling that your Goal is just before you, but that you are not able to see it. If you all the time feel that your Goal is in easy reach but that you do not know where it is, you will desperately cry for it, and naturally you will make an attempt to reach the Goal. Then, while you are making the attempt, automatically your inner being is flooded with dynamism.

If you feel that your Goal is far, you become relaxed and feel that Eternity is at your disposal. Then your inner dynamism does not come to the fore. But if you feel that what you want to grow into is just around the corner, only you have to use your conscious awareness to grasp it and claim it, then you will get dynamism. At that time, you will be constantly breathing in, consciously or unconsciously, the breath or soul of your Goal, and dynamism will be yours.

Dynamism means the death of your lethargic life, the death of your ignorance-life. The moment dynamism comes to the fore, immediately you see the death of lethargy, ignorance and anything else that

155

prevents you from reaching your Goal, growing into your Goal and becoming your Goal.

> The winter of your body's Lethargy
> Can immediately be over
> Only if you are ready to welcome
> The spring of your soul's dynamism.

Self-Indulgence

Self-control means wisdom-light.
Wisdom-light drinks deep the delight
Of the ever-transcending Beyond.

In comparison with insincerity, impurity, doubt and other weak-nesses, obstacles and negative qualities, self-indulgence is an almost incurable disease. I am not trying to discourage you; it is my business only to encourage you. But while encouraging you with all my heart, I have to say that self-indulgence lasts for a long, long, long time. After insincerity goes away, after impurity and doubt go away, you will see that self-indulgence still remains. Either in thought or in action, on the mental plane or the physical plane, self-indulgence will maintain its abode in the outer consciousness.

The spiritual seeker one day has to conquer self-indulgence, because God will not allow anybody to remain always self-indulgent. To be cured of self-indulgence, we need tremendous aspiration, con-stant aspiration, in addition to the divine Grace. It is very easy for us to say that by the Grace of God everything is possible. We have heard this and it is true. But this Grace does not come for all and sundry. This Grace comes only for those who really want to bask in its sun-shine. If we are prepared to run the fastest and offer what we have and what we are, if at every moment we are ready to offer everything for God, then nothing remains incurable for us. God wants perfection from each individual on earth. It is a matter of time, and that time God has chosen for us.

157

Everything in God's creation
Is temporary,
Save and except peace, love,
Joy and light.

A Special Aim

I wish to cite a few words from Sanskrit: *Sannyasa koru karma sadhana*. It means: "We have to practise the inner life, spiritual discipline, here inside the body. Here inside the body we have to live the life of the spirit."

Unfortunately, we either give undue importance to the body or we give it no importance at all. We must not be overly attached to the body. When we use the body for the sake of enjoyment, sense-pleasure, only to covet, we are misusing it. Again, if we offer contempt to the body, the physical consciousness, we will never be totally fulfilled here on earth. It is here on earth that we have to realise the Truth, fulfil the Truth and manifest the Truth.

Only if I can say that the soul is my own, only if I become inseparably one with my soul, will I see the purpose, the aim of my life. Why have I come here? What will God do through me here on earth? I live on earth precisely because I have a special aim, a mission. Everyone needs to feel that they have something special to offer, and this message has to come directly from the soul and enter into the physical consciousness.

Weakness Versus Strength

As an unlit individual, I boast, I brag. I say, "I have tremendous strength." But when an insignificant ant bites me, I am unnerved,

I am irritated. A mere mosquito disturbs my inner poise. I have the strength to destroy hundreds and thousands of mosquitoes, but I am conquered by a little mosquito or an ant. Why? Precisely because I live in the body.

We make ourselves feel that we are stronger than the senses, but the senses are really stronger than we are. Unless and until we have realised the highest Truth, the senses are infinitely more powerful. They are compelling us to do what they want. But if we live in the soul, then the senses are under our control. If we live in the soul, if our consciousness becomes totally one with the soul, which is the source of light and delight, then mosquitoes can bite, ants can bite; the whole world, like a venomous snake, can bite. We will remain unperturbed; we will remain in the sea of silence and tranquillity.

Let us look at self-indulgence as something that we think is very insignificant or very easy to conquer, but that we are allowing to enter into us. Some people say, "I smoke, true, but I can easily stop smoking." In this way they go on for months and years. They can conquer smoking, they say, but after twenty years they see how difficult it is. They do not, they cannot stop.

When people surrender to their weaknesses, we see how they ruin their lives. One philosophy is that we shall only pray and meditate on God, and God will take care of the rest of the world. But again, we can also look around; we can watch others and learn from their experiences. Let us say that I want to touch fire because I feel that fire is so charming. But if I see that somebody else has touched fire and his hand is now burnt, why shall I also do the same thing? Has God not shown me that someone else has burnt his fingers by touching fire? We can see what happens when others allow weakness to control them. Weakness itself is power, negative power. We have to use the positive strength to conquer our weakness, and that positive strength is our love of God. That is the only way.

159

There is no such thing
As a fruitful self-enjoyment.
There is no such thing
As a fruitful self-denial.
There is only one thing
Eternally fruitful:
God-acceptance in all.

A Powerful Antidote

Often when we are unable to conquer our weaknesses, it is because we are actually cherishing them. Outwardly, we want to destroy all the weaknesses that we see in ourselves, but inwardly, secretly, we enjoy them. This moment we take a weakness as our enemy, but the next moment we take it as our friend. In our outer life, our weakness is torturing us; but in our inner life – unconsciously, not consciously – we cherish this weakness.

Now, how do we cope with this situation? By remaining in the soul and not allowing dark forces to enter into us. How can we remain in the soul? Through our purity and our constant vigilance. Like a guard or a sentinel we have to stand right in front of our heart's door and prevent the undivine forces from entering. Only the divine forces of peace, light, bliss and delight shall we allow to come in. Then we will see that the life of self-indulgence gives way to the life of self-realisation and fulfilment.

Is there anything else that can cure our weaknesses? There is a medicine, an antidote, and that is our love-power. Our love-power for whom? Our love-power not for any individual, but for our Source, who is God. The stronger we can make our love for God, for our Source, the easier it is for us to conquer our weaknesses.

Surrender to your higher life.
Your lower life will be blessed
With a beautiful Smile
From God,
And your higher life will be blessed
With a new Message
From God.

Pleasure Versus Joy

We have to know that here on earth there is one thing called pleasure, another thing called joy. Unfortunately, some people make an Himalayan mistake when they think that pleasure is a form of joy. We observe that a child sometimes eats mud, dirt, rocks and all kinds of things. To him that is most delicious food. But when he grows up, he eats only real food. Similarly, when a person is not fully mature in the spiritual life, he indulges in undivine things. But when he makes inner progress, he sees that what he used to eat was all dirt and impurity, and he loses his taste for these things. When an aspirant begins to have significant, fulfilling inner experiences, his entire being is flooded with light and delight. At that time he can clearly see and feel the difference between physical pleasure and spiritual joy between mud and real food.

The human world, the outer consciousness, is crying for pleasure, and each time pleasure is fulfilled, we see that frustration looms large inside of it. When we buy something unnecessary like a Cadillac, soon afterwards we are frustrated because the one we have got is not big enough; we want something more comfortable. Comfort and pleasure go together. There are two Indian words: *aram*, meaning "comfort", and *haram*, meaning "very dangerous and destructive". India's Prime Minister Nehru used to say, "*Aram* is *haram*." Comfort

161

seems like something mild, but it is basically the same thing as plea-sure in the form of passion and is inevitably followed by destruction. If we run after comfort with the help of our desire, then naturally we will not be satisfied.

The physical is not and cannot be satisfied with its own posses-sions. It feels that others have the truth, light, beauty and bliss, whereas it does not. The very nature of the physical is to feel that it is the eternal beggar. It wants something from somewhere else, either from human beings or from Heaven. The soul is not like that. The soul constantly feels that it has everything from God in infinite measure, and that it has the potentiality to house Infinity. It is satis-fied with its reality because it knows what it has and what it can grow into. The very nature of the soul is to remain satisfied. It lives in divine satisfaction.

May each dream of our soul
Find its complete fulfilment
On earth.

Emotions

The most predominant emotion is the vital emotion, but emotion can also be in the body, in the mind and in the heart. Emotion in the body usually degrades our consciousness. Emotion in the impure heart blinds and binds us. When we say, "He is an emotional fellow," we are often referring to a person's undisciplined and unillumined vital emotion.

With our human emotion we possess and are possessed. But human emotion we have to transform and illumine. As night has to be trans-formed into light, so also human emotion has to be transformed into divine emotion.

Emotion in the pure heart illumines us and liberates us. Divine emotion says, "I am God's child. It is beneath my dignity to surrender myself to ignorance. My Father is all Light, all Perfection, all Love." This emotion comes directly from the inmost recesses of our heart.

If there is no effort to transform the vital emotional life into the purest spiritual life, then all of our spiritual activities will be a kind of self-deception, and in self-deception there is no God-realisation. When we use our emotions for enjoyment or self-indulgence, then we are ruining our inner life, but it is good if we can transform our vital emotions into divine joy, a divine emotion. If we use our emotions for inner determination, for self-liberation, then emotions are the strongest power in us. We can use them in this way, as our inner assistants.

Whenever emotion comes to the fore, do not try to suppress it. Just try to think of divine emotion. When we can expand ourselves totally, when we can remain in Infinity, in the Vast, then there is no necessity to possess anything or to get limited pleasure. If we meditate on joy, divine joy, then automatically we will grow into that joy.

Do not suppress your shortcomings.
Your shortcomings have to be accepted,
Perfected
And finally emancipated.

The Supremacy Of The Soul

When we aspire, the soul tells us to do something and we do it. But when we are a victim to teeming desires, even when the soul tells us not to do something, we do not listen.

The soul will ultimately gain its rightful supremacy. What happens is this: a superior officer comes to an office for the first time to replace

163

someone who has left. At first, the ordinary minor clerks in the office mock him. They do everything wrong and refuse to listen to him. The superior observes this situation in the office, but he knows that he is above it all. Gradually he exercises his authority. When the minor clerks see his power, they are afraid and they listen to him.

Similarly, in the spiritual life, the soul tolerates everything in the beginning. The body, the vital and the mind are unruly members of the family. They mock and disobey the soul. The soul also waits for some time. In the beginning the soul remains the witness. It observes who is good and who is bad. The soul welcomes the good and divine members of the family who listen to it. To them it says, "Let us run together." As for the bad members of the family who are deliberately creating problems, the soul refers their case to the Supreme. One day the Supreme will say, "Now the time has come to show your divine light through your divine authority." That is God's Hour for the soul to dispel the darkness of millennia from the human consciousness.

My Lord,
If You really love me,
Then use Your Authority
At every moment
In everything that I do.

Lord Indra And His Consort

A good man and a bad man were neighbours. One day the bad man said, "You have to develop artistic qualities. You have to go to some good clubs and learn about culture, philosophy, spirituality and many other things." The good man was hesitant. He said, "No, no. For me it is better to stay at home and read religious and spiritual books."

The bad man said, "At least come to my club once and see what it is like. You are bound to learn quite a few things that are necessary in human life." The good man agreed, and together they went to a club. They read aloud from religious and spiritual books and discussed all kinds of things. After the discussion they started drinking. They had such wonderful cultural, religious, spiritual and philosophical discussions, and then they started drinking!

When the good man came home, his wife could not believe her eyes. She could not recognise her husband. She cried, "What have you done? What have you done? I cannot recognise you!"

He said, "I have drunk wine."

His wife became furious. "How could you do this?" she shouted.

The husband said, "My friend told me it is good. Lord Indra used to drink nectar. His nectar and our wine are the same thing."

The wife was extremely angry. "No, no, you cannot drink! You must not drink!"

The man said, "All right, I promise not to drink any more."

Alas, once you drink wine, you are caught. When his neighbour invited him to go to the club again, the man said, "My wife will be furious. What am I going to do?"

The friend asked, "Tell me frankly, did you enjoy it?"

"Yes, I enjoyed it, but now I will have a fight at home. I will have a war!"

The neighbour said, "No, no, no, this time nothing will happen. You just come with me. I assure you, nothing will happen."

The good man went to the club again. He enjoyed philosophical, spiritual and all other kinds of discussion. When, along with his friend, he came back home heavily drunk, his wife was waiting. She said, "You promised not to do this!" Then she announced that she wanted to leave him.

The good man said, "No, this time my promise is definitely sincere. I will never, never go there again!"

The wife said, "Why did you tell me a lie? You said last time that you would never go there again!" He replied, "But even Lord Indra himself told many lies." His wife said, "Are you another Indra that you can lie to your heart's content?"

The husband said, "Indra told many, many lies, and even stole a cow. I have never stolen anything, so Indra went one step ahead of me. Indra was a thief, whereas I am only a liar. Indra has taught us how to tell lies. If Indra, the cosmic god, can tell lies, what is wrong with a human being telling lies?"

The following day was a holiday for the husband, so he did not go to work. His wife was really devoted to him. Every morning she would cook breakfast, and later she would cook lunch and dinner. Usually she cooked breakfast around eight o'clock in the morning. But on this particular day it became eleven o'clock and then twelve o'clock, and still the wife had not made breakfast. What was she doing? She was sewing a garment for herself. Finally the husband asked their son to tell his mother that it was getting late and he was extremely hungry.

The mother said to her son, "Please, please, my son, my darling, do not be involved in our fight – only watch and enjoy what is going on."

Her son said, "I do not want to be involved in your quarrel, Mother. Please, you take care of it."

Soon it became one o'clock, then two o'clock. Still the wife was not giving her husband any food. He was getting furious and finally said, "What kind of wife are you?"

His wife said, "Since you have become another Indra, I am definitely Sachi, Indra's wife. Who can tell me that Sachi ever cooked? She had many, many servants and maids to cook for her. I am Sachi now, so I do not need to cook any more. As you have become another Indra, you can have some cooks to prepare your food and some maids to serve you. Let them cook and serve you, because from now on, I will do whatever I want to do; I am a queen. After all, Indra was a king, and a king has all kinds of cooks and servants. I am a queen, so I will do whatever I like. I am not going to cook for you any more."

The man was so sad and disturbed to hear his wife's words. He said, "I will never, never go with my friend to that club again. I will remain devoted and faithful to you. This is absolutely my solemn promise."

Their son was overjoyed that his parents had become reconciled. From that day on, the wife cooked and did everything for her husband, as usual, and her husband kept his promise. He did not go to that club any more. This was how the wife taught her husband a lesson.

God is keeping His Promise.
He is holding you up
Carefully and firmly
And keeping you from swaying.
Perhaps you, too,
Made a solemn promise to God.
Perhaps!

The Middle Path

In the spiritual life, the most important, significant and fruitful thing is self-control. No self-control, no self-realisation. In the dictionary we come across hundreds of thousands of words. Of all these words, self-control is the most difficult one to practise. How can we have self-control? We have to surrender ourselves to the Source. This Source is Light; this Source is God.

How can we inspire the body, the vital, the mind and the heart to enter into better and more fulfilling light? If we find fault with them, we can never change and transform them. But if we appreciate them, saying that they have the capacity to play a significant role in God's cosmic Drama, that they are as important as the soul for the full manifestation of God on earth, then we can transform them. If we do not condemn the body, vital, mind and heart – on the contrary, if we tell them that they can be the chosen instruments of God, that God needs them for His divine *Lila* or Game on earth – then eventually we can transform them. The unruly members of our family will before long feel the importance of their respective roles in the fulfilment of God's manifestation. They can and will be unified for the fulfilment of a single goal.

Self-control takes time. It cannot be achieved overnight. Through introspection, self-examination and proper meditation, one achieves it. Again, self-control does not mean self-torture. Neither does it mean austerity. Unfortunately, in the West, self-control has been misunderstood. People think that the austere, arduous life practised by some Indian aspirants of the past stands as the ideal of self-control. But that kind of austere life, torturing and punishing the body, is not real self-control. It is self-mortification. If somebody wants to realise God by fasting for days and months, then he will be embraced by death, not by God.

A normal, natural life – the middle path – is what God demands from us. The Buddha taught us to follow the middle path, not to go to extremes. We have to be very firmly planted on earth. The root of the tree is under the ground, and the branches are looking up towards the highest. Self-control is within and self-manifestation is without. Today's self-control will be tomorrow's self-transcendence.

I wish to tell about an incident in the life of Socrates. Once Socrates and a host of admirers went to see a palmist. The palmist read Socrates' hand and said, "What a bad person you are, ugly and full of lower vital problems. Your life is full of corruption." Socrates' admirers were thunderstruck. They wanted to strike the palmist. What gall he had to say such things about Socrates, who was truly a pious man, a saint!

But Socrates said, "Wait, let us ask him if he has said everything." Then the palmist continued, "No, I have something more to say. This man has all these undivine qualities, without doubt, but he has not shown any of them. They are all under his control."

There is but one philosophy:
God can be seen
With my aspiration-cry.
There is but one religion:
My life's sunrise begins
With God's Compassion-Beauty.
There is but one code of life:
I live to love God.
God lives to purify me and perfect me,
So that He can hoist His Victory-Banner
In the battlefield of my life.

Fixing Our Mind On God

When we try to conquer the senses by force, by suppression, we are taking the negative path. By beating or striking our desires we can never get joy; only by pouring illumination into them can we get real joy. If we suppress something today, then tomorrow there will be an inner revolt. By suppressing something, what are we doing? We are only forcing ourselves beyond our inner willingness. It is just a kind of desire that we have. "I shall control my senses. I shall conquer my passions." This approach cannot bring us what we actually want. The hungry lion that lives in our senses and the hungry tiger that lives in our passions will not leave us because of the mere repetition of this thought.

What we must do is fix our mind on God. To our utter amazement, our lion and tiger, now tamed, will leave us of their own accord when

169

they see that we have become too poor to feed them. But we have not become poor in the least. On the contrary, we have become infinitely stronger and richer, for God's Will energises our body, mind and heart. To fix our body, mind and heart on the Divine is the right approach. The closer we are to the Light, the farther we are from the darkness.

Hidden Treasure

In the spiritual life, the role of discipline is most significant. An aspirant is spiritual just because he knows the meaning of self-discipline. Discipline is our inner awareness of Truth. Discipline is the total purification of our outer life.

There are two Sanskrit words: *abhyasa* and *vairagya*. *Abhyasa* means practise. If you want to practise the spiritual life, you need to meditate every day. Just as every day you eat to feed your outer body, so every day you need to feed the soul, the divine child in you, through your aspiration.

Vairagya means discretion and indifference to the gross earthly life. You have to feel that the world of pleasure is not for you. The world of joy, the world of delight is for you. Whenever you choose pleasure, you have to know that it will be followed by frustration. But joy and delight constantly grow in your inner nature and outer life as you practise spiritual disciplines.

The Sanskrit word *dama* means control of the senses. We start there. Another word, *shama*, means control of desire and thought. A third is *shama dama*, control of the intellect. The intellect has to be transcended. If we do not put an end to our teeming, fruitless desires and to the life of our doubting, unfortunate mind, and if we do not go far beyond the domain of the spiritually barren intellect with its pride, vanity and dance of ego, then we can never hope to discover the hidden treasure deep within us.

Discipline and its practise are like the obverse and reverse of the same coin. We cannot separate discipline from practise; they have to go together. When we practise the spiritual life, God practises something in us and for us – the game of His boundless Compassion.

Nobody can change.
Nobody will change.
But you can and you shall.

Nobody can smile.
Nobody will smile.
But you can and you shall.

Prove to the world within,
Prove to the world without
That you are God's choicest instrument
Unparalleled.

Bitter Medicine Or Reality-Delight?

Whenever we want to do something, immediately the mind vetoes it. Even if the mind itself wanted it two days ago or two years ago, the mind is now ready to veto that same thing. Right now when we think of discipline, we feel that it is nothing short of punishment, precisely because of the mind's unwillingness.

Instead, we have to feel that discipline is our help, our guide, our inspiration, our aspiration, even our realisation. It is discipline that can and will conquer the undivine forces in and around us. Let us think of discipline as a new master who is helping us to learn something new, meaningful, soulful and fruitful, so that we will not have to learn anything more from our old master. Our old master was lethargy, darkness, ignorance and all the other negative forces. Now we have to give the utmost value to our new master, discipline.

In India, how I suffered from malaria! You cannot imagine how painful it is. All the nerves start dancing. Such pain! You simply shout and scream. Previously perhaps you did not know any acrobatics or special exercises, but as soon as you get malaria you become an expert. Pain compels you to do so.

The only medicine for malaria is quinine. It is extremely bitter – no other medicine is as bitter. But quinine is the saviour. If we do not accept the medicine, then how are we going to get rid of our fever? Knowledge comes in the form of discipline, which is like quinine. If we accept this discipline, then only can we conquer our ignorance. Discipline embodies light, and it is more than eager to offer us light. Only if we can feel this, will we be unafraid of discipline. What the mind calls discipline, the heart calls a process by which we achieve something or gain something. The soul does not even call it a process. The soul feels that what we call discipline not only embodies reality-delight but is reality-delight itself.

A disciplined life
Is a favourite instrument
Of God.

Will-Power

It is very easy for us to use the term "struggle", but we have to know whether it is a real inner struggle. If a lazy person has to budge an inch, he calls it a struggle. If we have to get up early in the morning, we say that it is a struggle.

We want to achieve our goal with determined personal efforts, supported and guided by God's loving Grace. But at times we find it difficult to separate our willing from our wishing. Whenever we will to achieve something, we pay the price, whereas when we wish to achieve something, very often we do not pay the price: we just wish. Here there is no conscious effort, and so we can hardly expect any success.

Will-power is an ever-progressive and self-manifesting reality in the universe. What is will-power? It is our conscious inner urge to enter into the very heart of Infinity, Eternity and Immortality. To live a devoted life is to be a conscious child of God's Will. The difference between determination and divine will-power is this: determination is in the mind; divine will-power is in the soul. Because the mind is very limited, mental determination is not enduring; it is all fluctuation. Mental determination is constantly being destroyed, since the mind accepts different ideas at every moment. But the will of the soul is everlasting, ever-progressing and ever-fulfilling because it is one with the Will of the Supreme.

Each individual has to realise within himself what true struggle is. The real struggle for a sincere seeker is to conquer ignorance in his own life and in the world around him. We have to know how hard we are trying to realise the Highest, how many minutes of our daily life we are consecrating to the Supreme in us, how much we are struggling to see the Light within us and within others. If we are sincerely struggling to conquer ourselves, if we are sincerely struggling against falsehood, inertia, darkness, imperfection, limitation and bondage, then our very effort is bound to give us joy.

Who asks you to walk
Through an endless darkness-tunnel?
Do you not see that the road of light
Can easily be part and parcel
Of your life's treasure trove?

Sacrifice – The Choices We Make

Let us consider sacrifice in our ordinary day-to-day lives. Suppose you are a student. You want to study in the evening at seven o'clock for your examination. You want to prepare yourself to pass the examination, but exactly at seven o'clock there is a wonderful movie playing. If you go to the movie, then naturally you will be sacrificing your studies. In the ordinary life you will say that this is not a sacrifice; you feel like going to a movie and you just go. But no! If you become sincere, you will see that you have made a sacrifice of the time that you were going to use for your studies. If, instead of going to the movie, you study at home seriously and devotedly, you sacrifice two hours of your pleasure in order to prepare for your examination.

At every moment we get the opportunity to sacrifice. What are we going to sacrifice? We do not have to sacrifice our body, our home, our parents, our children and family. Sacrifice means that we have to give up the things which are not opening to the light.

There are many things wrong with us; we have darkness, imperfection and limitation inside us. We have to sacrifice them consciously to the light within us. From the spiritual point of view, sacrifice means the renunciation of our ignorance, our weakness, our bondage.

Sacrifice involves the total being: the body, the vital, the mind, the heart and the soul. In the spiritual life, sacrifice means that all that we have and all that we are, in our entire being, must be dedicated to the highest and deepest in us. At that time, the body will not have its own individuality; it will be the conscious play of the Divine in us. The mind will not have its own individuality. The mind and vital will also be conscious instruments of the Divine.

Sacrifice does not mean that, by giving, we lose something. We sacrifice our limited self to our highest and largest Self, and at that time we immediately become the largest and the highest Self. When we offer something to the Divine with our mind, heart and soul, we actually become the Divine in our entire being. We sacrifice the hunger of our body and the demands of our mind to our heart and soul. This sacrifice is not something mental. When we can sacrifice our entire being, we feed the Divine in ourselves.

Again, when we go deep into the inmost recesses of our soul, we feel there is no such thing as sacrifice. When we use this term, we must see that in it is the fulfilment of our conscious will. Sacrifice, in the purest sense of the term, is a conscious way of becoming one with our own highest, with the all-pervading Consciousness of the Absolute Supreme.

Each individual
Has entered into the world
For a special fulfilment
Of God's Will.

Life-Mastery

The highest Truth can be realised only here on earth. God-discovery and self-realisation can take place only here on earth. The soul is inside the body. Now it is the light of the soul that has to come to the fore to illumine the obscure, unlit, undivine consciousness. Once our outer consciousness is illumined, only then is there no difference between the inner and the outer. Unless and until the inner realisation and the outer life's manifestation go together, we will remain incomplete. Take the body as the field of manifestation. If we have realised something and we cannot manifest it, then the Truth is incomplete.

Unfortunately, we are living in an age when self-control is not appreciated. It has become an object of ridicule. If someone is trying hard for self-mastery, his friends, neighbours, relatives and acquaintances all mock him. They find no reality in his sincere attempt to master his life. They think that the way they are living their lives is more worthwhile. According to them, the man who is trying to control his life is a fool. But who is the fool – he who wants to conquer himself or he who is constantly a victim of fear, doubt, worry and anxiety? Needless to say, he who wants to conquer himself is not only the wisest person but the greatest divine hero.

Try to be sincere with yourself. Let the world find fault with you. Let the world bark at you. Your sincerity is your safeguard. Your spiritual discipline will lead you to your destined Goal. Who is the king? Not he who governs a country, but he who has conquered himself.

Self-mastery and God-discovery
Are the only two things
That each human being on earth
Must take seriously.
Everything else can be taken lightly.

Part Four

The Supreme Commander

Faith

In the inner world
I can have sunshine every day,
For my inner faith is founded upon
God's infallible Promise-Light.

Faith is a gift. Every good quality is a gift from God. But faith you can also develop. Today you have a little faith; tomorrow you will have more. Again, faith is like a box with a jewel inside. You have the box, but you are not opening it in order to see the jewel. If you go to the Source, you will see that you have faith in infinite measure.

Faith and spirituality are inseparable. They are like a farmer and a field. Spirituality is the field and faith is the farmer. One without the other is useless. There is a fixed hour when God will kindle our consciousness whether we have faith in Him or not. He waits for the choice hour, and when the hour strikes, He comes and gives us what He wants to give. But that does not mean that we shall not aspire, that we shall live in the world of sleep and not make any personal effort. No! We shall go on like a true farmer and cultivate the soil with sincere dedication and regularity, and after we do our part, we will leave it up to God to decide when He wants to give us the bumper crop of realisation.

Faith is a transforming experience and not just an idea. Faith has the magic key to self-discovery. Self-discovery is the bona fide discovery of Reality. Faith is an active participant in divine love, harmony and peace.

The role of faith is of paramount importance in the seeker's life. What you call faith, I call the soul's foreknowledge of the highest

179

Truth. Faith tells the aspirant not only what God is, but also what God can do for him at every moment. This faith is the aspirant's living breath in God the Omniscient and God the Omnipotent.

Have faith in yourself.
You will have a new heart of assurance.
Have faith in God.
You will have a new life of accomplishment.

The Faith-Entrance

There are people who mock faith. But faith is the eye that sees the future in the immediacy of the present. When we have faith in the spiritual life, we do not stumble, we do not walk, we do not march. We simply run the fastest. If we have implicit faith in God, the Inner Pilot, and in our own aspiration, then we constantly run the fastest towards our destined Goal.

Some people, especially those who do not have a very developed intellect or sophisticated mind, spontaneously have faith. When the mind is very powerful and predominant, it is difficult to have faith in God, because the mind sees thousands of doors that lead into God's Palace, whereas the heart sees only one. When the mind starts to enter into God's Palace, it tries to see whether this door is good or that other one. It comes near one door and then it thinks that perhaps the other door is better. So it goes here and there, trying all the doors, and it takes a long time to enter. But the wise heart knows only one door, and that door is faith, absolute faith. Through this door it immediately enters into God's Palace.

Again, even if you are intellectually developed, that does not mean that you cannot also have faith in God. If your heart is also developed, the conviction of the heart is reflected in the mind. First of all, faith is not credulity or blind belief. It does not mean that you must constantly believe in the impossible. No, faith is a spontaneous feeling. It does not care for human justification. It is the eye that envisions the future and is always in tune with a higher truth. The door of faith is always open to the Truth and, by virtue of faith, we transcend ourselves.

If something is true, you will feel it within the very depths of your heart. But sometimes it may take a little time. You sow a seed. After a few months it germinates. In a year it grows into a sapling, and eventually it grows into a huge tree. When you begin to take an interest in the spiritual life, you have only sown the seed. You may not see the results immediately. You will feel light and peace, but first you have to have faith.

To increase strength, inner and outer,
What we need is more faith,
And nothing else.

Inner Perception

Inside you there are many organs: heart, lungs and so on. Although you cannot see these things, you know that they are there. Similarly, in the inner world, if you do not see something right now, that does not mean that it does not exist.

You have to start with faith – sincere, genuine, sublime faith. This faith is not going to mislead you. When you read a spiritual book, that book embodies light. While reading, you may not feel light inside the book right away, but still you do not discard the book. You have faith in the messages that it contains. You meditate on the words and ideas that the book embodies, and eventually you do get light. Inside the book there is a hidden reality. If you believe in that hidden reality

181

while you are reading, in the course of time you will get illumination. But you have to read the book in order to get its essence.

Similarly, you have to pray and meditate before you will feel your own divinity. If you cannot feel it right now, do not be sad or upset. Pray and meditate sincerely, and through your faith, your real divinity will one day loom large. If you do not have higher experiences or realisations as soon as you enter into the spiritual life, do not give up. Right now if you do not feel inside the very depths of your heart something divine, illumining, fulfilling and perfect, no harm. It takes time to acquire a free access to the inner world. But once you have free access to the inner world, you will see that it is flooded with light and delight.

> My Lord, I see Your Smile-River
> Flowing across my eyes.
> Can I not show You
> Soulfully and unconditionally
> My heart's dance of flame-delight?

Faith And Receptivity

Any aspect of God is bound to transform one's life. It is the seeker who has to have boundless faith in some aspect of God. It can be the Power aspect, the Peace aspect, the Love aspect, the Light aspect or any aspect. It is up to the seeker to develop faith, absolute faith, in any aspect of God.

When calling on the Supreme, you have to know in which word you have more faith. When one person says "God", all his love, faith and devotion come to the fore. For someone else, this may not be so.

God is beyond our doubt and faith. If we doubt God, it does not affect Him. But if we love God and if we have faith in Him, then it becomes infinitely easier for us to receive His Love, Affection, Compassion and Joy. If I need ten dollars, but I doubt that my friend has any money at all, then how am I going to get money from him? I will not even ask him. But if I have faith that he has a hundred dollars or even more, and that he will give me something because I am asking him, then definitely he will give it to me. Similarly, if we doubt that God exists, or if we doubt what He has to offer us, then we will not ask Him for any of His divine qualities. If we doubt that God is good, why should we ask God to make us good or to make us happy?

> *Do you know that your world*
> *Is not God's entire world?*
> *Do you know that God's entire world*
> *Can house your world?*
> *Do you know that your world*
> *Can claim anything from God's world*
> *As its very own?*

Return To Childhood

Whatever the physical mind wants to see, it sees in an infinitesimal part. It always divides, breaks and kills the entirety, the wholeness of the Truth. The very function of the physical mind is to limit the Truth, the Light, or whatever can uplift your heart and soul. It has to make the Truth very tiny so that it can see and appreciate it.

Whether it is the intellectual mind or the ordinary mind, the mind has its own way of doubting, suspecting and doing all kinds of undivine things. Even if you are very mature, very developed in the spiritual life, the best thing is to think that you are four years old. If you think that you are a child, then you make the fastest progress. A child has immediate receptivity because he does not rely on his own capacity. He relies on his mother. Again, he is eager to give his little capacity, which is his faith. You can also become a child just by unlearning. Ignorance and darkness have taught you many things which you can now unlearn.

If you can have the kind of implicit faith that you had in your childhood, then you will again be fulfilled. When you were a child, the moment you saw that your mother was not near or around you, you felt helpless. In the spiritual life also, when you have the inner guidance, the guidance of a Master or the Supreme, then you feel safe. When you miss or lose that inner guidance, you feel unsafe. Your spiritual Master will not deceive you; your Inner Pilot will not deceive you.

Give What You Have

In the spiritual life, if you can please your inner being, your soul, your Inner Pilot, your spiritual Master, with your limited capacity, then you will see that the object of your adoration is bound to give you something far beyond your imagination.

You give a little aspiration during your prayer or meditation for a few minutes early in the morning. Then immediately your spiritual Master or God will invoke so many things for you: peace, light, bliss, joy and delight. God will never be indebted to you. The moment He sees that you are regular in your meditation, that you are sincere and earnest and that you have accepted this approach to the spiritual life wholeheartedly, God showers His boundless Compassion on you in the form of light, delight and peace. Give to God what you have: your childlike faith and inner cry.

My Supreme,
What do You see in me?
"My child, I see in you

184

What you never see –
Your implicit inner oneness
With My Heart."

Claim Your Inheritance

Once faith is lost, it is almost impossible to get it back. Once you lose faith in a spiritual Teacher, in an ordinary human being or even in an idea, you will have to suffer for a long, long time before you get it back. But if you lose faith in yourself, then you have lost everything. You are worse than a street beggar. If you have faith in yourself, then you can ultimately become divine. But if you do not have faith even in yourself, your case is really hopeless. It is useless to have faith in God, whom most of us think is in Heaven, if you do not have faith in yourself on earth.

You have to have faith that you can realise God. You have to have faith that you can be the possessor of infinite Light, Peace and Bliss. You have to have faith in your aspiration, in your concentration, in your meditation and contemplation. Only then will the goal of God-realisation and the divinisation of human nature and earth-consciousness become yours.

You have to know that you are God's child and not God's slave. If you feel that God is the Lord and you are His slave, then how are you going to have faith in yourself? A slave will immediately say, "Today he is my master. Tomorrow he may kick me out." A slave cannot claim his master's wealth or capacity as his very own, but a child can.

If you want to have faith in yourself, first you have to feel what kind of connection or relationship you have established with your Inner Pilot. If it is the relationship of Father and son, or Mother and son, or lover and Beloved, if it is the relationship of two most intimate, absolutely closest friends, then you can expect anything from Him. But if you cannot establish that kind of sweet oneness between yourself and God, then how will you have faith? If you think, "He is very aloof; He is the Lord Supreme and I am just a meaningless creature," then there is no feeling of oneness.

If you think of yourself as a tiny ant and God as a huge elephant, then naturally you will say, "Oh, how can I have such strength, such capacity? I am so weak and insignificant." But if you think of God as someone who is more than eager to give you what He has, then you will feel, "The strength that that elephant has is all for me when the time comes or when I need it." When you have established that kind of feeling, when you feel that your Father is going to give you every-thing that you need, then automatically you will have faith. In the spiritual life, always try to feel your oneness with God as something extremely sweet, pure and fulfilling. Then automatically you get faith. If you feel, "He is mine and I am His," then automatically you will have abundant faith in yourself.

> *Deepen your faith in yourself.*
> *Nothing will be able to frighten*
> *Or weaken you.*

Faith In A Spiritual Teacher

If you have faith in anybody or anything, then you should increase your faith and dedicate your life to that person or that ideal. If you have faith in a teacher, then you should try to increase it. On earth there are many teachers. If you have faith in a particular teacher, then that is the one you should follow. At that time you do not have to ask somebody else.

Absence of doubt is one thing, but faith, real faith, is something else. There are many people who do not doubt the capacity of a spiritual Master, but they do not have faith in him either. They do not doubt his spiritual height, but that does not mean that they are going to have infinite faith in what he advises them to do in their business life or their mental life. These are two different things altogether. I may not have doubt, but I may have a neutral feeling. My sympathetic feeling towards a spiritual Master does not mean that I will go and touch his feet.

A real spiritual Teacher will say that he is not the Guru; the only real Guru is the Supreme. A human being is only a leader for a few people. It may be a hundred people or a thousand, or it may be millions. But the real Guru, the only real Guru, is God. If you accept a human being as your Guru, it is just because he is more illumined than you are.

If the Guru, the human teacher, is sincere and illumined, then he is getting light directly from the Supreme. He should then be considered as the higher part of the seeker, not as a different person. Since the physical feels that the mind is superior, the physical listens to the mind. Similarly, if the seeker feels that the person whom he has accepted as his Guru has more wisdom-light than he does, then he listens to that person, not with a sense of separativity, but as he would listen to his own highest part.

A spiritual Teacher is like the elder brother in the family. The elder ones in the family generally know more than the younger ones, so they are in a position to show the younger ones where the goal is. Once they do this, then their job is over.

We cannot consciously remain in our own highest consciousness all the time, but if we know that there is someone who always represents or embodies our highest part, then we can easily listen to him. If my head tells my legs to do something, my legs do not constantly question the wisdom or truth of my head's directions. I do not feel that it is beneath their dignity to do what my head tells them, because I know that my head and my legs are part and parcel of my own body. In the same way, the Guru and his disciples are inseparably one.

> A true truth-seeker and God-lover
> Is he whose outer and inner life
> Are powerfully anchored
> Inside his heart's starlit faith.

Swimming In The Sea of Delight

When we are worried or afraid of something, we immediately try to create a kind of self-imposed faith in God. This is not true faith. When we are in danger, we say, "God, save me, save me!" But we say this only to avert danger. It is an escape. This kind of faith does not last.

Everything is inside a person, both joy and fulfilment. But who is the possessor of this inner fulfilment? It is God. We are just His devoted instruments. When we feel spontaneous inner joy as part and parcel of our life, and we feel its source, then we can have faith in God.

Try to feel from now on that there is Somebody who does not want anything from you except joy. There is Somebody who wants you always to swim in the sea of joy and delight. If you can remain in joy – I do not mean the outer joy of going here and there, mixing with people, buying material things, but in real joy and inner fulfilment – then you will automatically have faith in God. In regard to your outer frustrations, try to separate your inner joy from these outer happenings. If you soulfully meditate and unconditionally surrender your day-to-day existence to the Almighty, then delight will be your inner reality. Your outer experience may be otherwise;

it may seem painful or destructive. But in your inner experience you shall become inseparably one with the cosmic Will. In that Will there is no suffering.

Since God Himself has created
My God-hunger,
I am sure He will definitely bring me
The greatest meal.

Kindling The Faith-Flame

You can develop more faith, abundant faith and boundless faith by mixing with someone who already has this faith. It is like mixing with a person who has more knowledge than you have; it brings to the fore your own knowledge. Similarly, if you feel that somebody has more faith in God than you, then it is advisable to mix with him. When someone has more faith than you have, your faith-flame will be kindled. Even if you do not get the opportunity to talk to him all the time, his very presence in silence will increase the faith within you. Unconsciously your heart will be able to draw, like a magnet, aspiration, peace and other divine qualities from him.

It is always advisable for seekers to mix with other seekers, for then they will be inspired. If you stay with somebody who is not aspiring at all, that means you are constantly struggling. It is very difficult for a seeker – especially in the beginning – to maintain his highest consciousness. As soon as he goes somewhere, immediately he comes into contact with unaspiring people. Even if he does not talk to them, still their vibration is affecting him. If you meet a saint, immediately you will feel his vibration. And if you meet a thief, immediately you will feel that vibration. But if you are a seeker and another seeker is with you, then immediately your strength increases tremendously. It is always advisable for seekers to be in a community together or to meet together often.

> It is the bounden duty
> Of the truth-seekers and God-lovers
> Of the New Millennium
> To transform the old decadence of the mind
> Into a new renaissance of the heart.

Faith's Clear Vision

Having faith in God is the perfect answer to all questions. But our faith has to be something inner and deep. It is not mere outer confidence. This faith is the river that is flowing into the sea of ever-growing, ever-illumining reality.

People who only believe what they see with their naked eyes are only eating half the fruit. If you want to scrutinise the Truth, to see whether it has a tail or a nose, then you will lose it. Truth is a matter of identification. This is the Christ's pronouncement about faith and doubt: Blessed are those who have faith without demanding proof at every moment.

When you live in the ordinary world, the unaspiring world, you have to see in order to believe. But when you aspire, first you believe the Truth and then you see the Truth. You have faith in something, and your faith is the precursor of your seeing. Normally we say, "Seeing is believing." But if you believe in something, then you can say that believing is seeing.

You are the instrument of God. If you have faith in your own life, in the life of aspiration, and if you have faith in divine Grace, then you can say that you are going to see, feel and become the Truth. Faith is the precursor of realisation. When you actually realise the

Truth, at that time you will see that realisation is totally one with faith. Faith sees what is coming ahead; faith becomes totally one with what you are going to realise.

The higher you go, the more clearly you will be able to see that faith is clearing the way. It is your own faith in yourself, in your spiritual Master, in God and in your life of aspiration that is hastening your realisation. What is realisation? Realisation means that you know you are not the finite, you are the Infinite. It is in the finite that the Infinite is playing its favourite tune. When the Infinite plays through the finite and uses the finite as its very instrument, and when the finite can claim the Infinite as its own in the field of realisation and in the field of manifestation, then only God the Infinite and God the finite become totally fulfilled in each other.

It was God's Plan
Right from the beginning of time
To give our soulful faith
A splendid victory.

The Real in Us

The more you love the divinity
Inside your life,
The sooner God's Reality
Will flower inside your heart.

God is One. At the same time, He is many. He is One in His highest Transcendental Consciousness. He is many here on earth in the field of manifestation. At the highest, He is unity. Here on earth, He is multiplicity. God is the lotus, and He has many, many petals, each representing an individual aspect of Himself. He is manifesting Himself in infinite ways and in infinite forms.

The lotus as a flower has its own individual identity, but each of its petals also has its own individuality. Some petals are small, some big, and each petal has its own shape. When we look at the petals of the lotus separately, we get tremendous joy because we are appreciating the individuality and the personality of each petal. At the same time, when we look at the flower as a whole, we appreciate the individuality and the personality of the entire lotus.

Each quality in our life, each capacity in our nature, is a kind of individuality and personality. Somebody can be a musician and also an architect, a carpenter and a cook. How many capacities one person can have! He is doing everything, but is it creating a conflict in his life? No. He is harmonising everything, because he knows that all these capacities are his and he claims them as his very own. If you take the capacities as individual factors in his life, then you will see that each capacity has its own individuality and personality. But since the individual can house all the capacities perfectly in his life, the music capacity will not be threatened by the carpentry capacity; they will go perfectly together. Similarly, in a group, somebody is a singer, somebody is a dancer, somebody is a poet; but they all harmonise. The group is only an extension of the individual's consciousness.

A piano has many keys. Each key has its distinct note or sound. When the keys are played together, they do not lose their individuality and personality, but they act as a unit and create something really special. In an orchestra, so many instruments are being played, and each instrument represents or embodies a kind of individuality and personality. When they are played together, they create such a divine atmosphere; they bring down Heaven on earth. Similarly, we expand and strengthen ourselves when we mix together.

> *Indeed, the choice*
> *Of humanity's divinity is perfect.*
> *It desires to see*
> *All seekers living together*
> *As good members*
> *Of a single world-community.*

Drops Entering The Ocean

Again, we do not have to lose our individuality and personality. Instead, we have to feel and realise our all-pervading divine individuality and all-serving divine personality. In our outer life we are filled with insecurity, jealousy, impurity, doubt and many other negative qualities. When we speak of individuality, we immediately think of all of these qualities. But there is another kind of individuality, the divine individuality, which is a direct expression of the Divine in us.

In our inner life we are all love for God and all concern for mankind. This inner life, which is the life of oneness, is our real life. now, we may only value our outer life, which is full of limitations and imperfections; we may not enter into our inner life to see who we actually are. We are like tiny drops. When a tiny drop enters into the ocean, it becomes part and parcel of the infinite ocean. Similarly, although we are all finite beings, when we lovingly, devotedly and unconditionally offer our limited existence to our Lord Supreme, out of His infinite Bounty, He makes us one, inseparably one, with His infinite Existence. The inner life of aspiration, dedication and realisation we must claim as our own, very own. If we can claim the inner life and inner reality as our own, then in the near or distant future, we will become exemplary human beings. How can we do this? Only by thinking of a oneness-heart, praying for a oneness-heart and actually living the life of a oneness-heart.

The deeper we go, the sooner we see that the real reality is within us, not without. Reality is the constant and dynamic process of our inner evolution. It is at once the expansion of our human consciousness and the essence of our divine consciousness. Human consciousness shakes hands with possibility and ability. Divine consciousness embraces faith and surrender.

The madness of this world
Cannot be conquered
By the sadness or the power
Of the world,
But only by the oneness
Of the world-hearts.

The One And The Many

Many years ago I wrote a play about Lord Krishna, and some of my students performed it. From the spiritual point of view, the actor who played Krishna held the highest part. He played his role extremely well and I was most proud of him. Krishna's friend Sudam, the most insignificant person, the poorest of all, also played his part well. Krishna was the king, the emperor, the Lord of the empire, the Lord of creation; and Sudam had no status at all. When they met, the friend had his own individuality and personality and Krishna also had his own status, but when both of them talked they became one. At that time I was not able to separate Sudam or anybody else in the play from Krishna. They went together. Everybody's personality and individuality all came together, and it became a grand play.

If we want to separate the characters, we can; one is Krishna, one is Arjuna, one is Sudam and so forth. But when they work together, they do not lose their personalities, their individualities. On the contrary, their personalities and individualities are strengthened because one person's force is entering into the other and vice versa. If we belong to the same family, then my strength will enter into you and it will increase your own individuality and personality, and your strength will enter into me. Or if my mind carries me to someone in India, my own individuality immediately becomes one with the person there. When my consciousness takes me into a person, I become part and parcel of him. This way I expand my consciousness.

In our true Self, we are all one. But in our outer self, we are many. Among the many, we see that one is serving the other. We always serve the moment we consciously enter into something other than ourselves. In this kind of service, my individuality remains inside you and your individuality remains inside me. It is in the extension of our personality in the form of this expanded individuality that the Supreme expresses Himself in infinite ways.

When I am in
My highest consciousness,
Everything feels like God
To me.

Grain And Gold

A human being is the embodiment, realisation and expression of Truth – the lesser Truth, the higher Truth and the highest Truth. Each moment the Divine is transcending its boundaries in us. We see it, feel it and realise it when we live the inner life, the life of the soul. How can we feel that the inner world is real? The reality of something depends on the importance or value we give to it.

Once there was a village zamindar who was nice, kind and honest. He had a lot of land and also a very large barn, where he used to keep grain. One day, while walking in front of his house, he saw a few pieces of grain on the ground. He bent down and started picking them up.

Two travellers happened to be passing by. They said, "We heard that you are a very, very rich man, a very kind man and a very generous man. What are you doing? Why are you not asking your servants to pick up these bits of grain? It is only a very few kernels – six or seven. It is not even worth asking your servants to do it. Why are you picking up this grain at all? On the one hand you are so generous, but now you are acting like a miserly man."

The zamindar said, "I am not miserly; I am generous. But why do I have to waste anything? I do not want to waste even a single kernel of grain. When it is necessary, I show my generosity. But when it is a

196

matter of being economical, why should I waste even one piece of grain? Today I will waste ten bits of grain, tomorrow twenty and the day after tomorrow many more."

One of the travellers said, "Yes, but we thought that you were collecting the pieces of grain as if they were the most precious jewellery, most precious gold coins. So inwardly we were laughing at you. But we see that you are right. It is good to be economical. Now we shall go."

The zamindar said, "Since you are passing by my house and you have said that I am kind and generous, let me be hospitable to you. Why not stay and eat with me, and then go?"

The travellers went to eat in the zamindar's house. He said to his guests, "Usually I do not serve anyone myself because I have so many servants. But I like you two; you seem to be very nice people. Let me serve you." Then the zamindar brought them a plate containing ten gold coins instead of food.

The travellers said to him, "What are you doing? How can we eat gold coins? Have you brought this by mistake or for some other special reason? Is it out of your generosity that you are doing this? You are really kind-hearted and compassionate. We are so grateful. But now we are very hungry. This is not the time to get gold coins. We cannot eat them."

The zamindar said, "Oh no, I am showing you two something. When I was collecting the pieces of grain, you laughed at me. You acted as though they were not valuable, whereas gold coins were valuable. I have brought you these gold coins to show you that every-thing has its own value at the proper time. Gold coins are valuable, true. But you cannot eat them. When you are hungry, you do not think of gold coins – you want to eat food. At that time, grain is even more precious than gold coins."

The Inner Reality

If we are hungry, immediately food becomes the only reality to us, around us, within us, without us. Anything that demands our attention or concentration has to be real, whether it is material food or inner peace, light and delight. The reality of something entirely depends on how necessary it is for us. If we need something, then that very thing has to become real.

When we do not pray and meditate, we see only the physical world around us. We feel that this is absolutely real. But when we pray and meditate, we see and feel that there is another world and that this physical world is only an expression of that world. But again, we have to know that we ourselves are the creator of this other world, just as we are the creator of this physical world. The physical world is like a house that we build with our hands, with our outer capacities. Similarly, the inner world we build with our will-power – not mere thought-power, but will-power. When we create something in the inner world with our will-power, if what we create is pure, divine and immortal, then we feel that we are safe.

The soul is inside the heart, and the heart is inside the body. To complete the game, we cannot remain inside the inner reality only. We have to come out to the outer reality. Otherwise, there will only be a tenant with no house to live in. Both the tenant and the house are equally important. If there is a tenant, only then will we feel the necessity of a house. Again, if there is a house, then we will definitely need a tenant. The soul is the tenant and the body is the house.

The inner world is real because we know everything that is within will one day come forth and blossom. The seed is under the ground, within Mother Earth. But one day it germinates and grows into a plant, a sapling and, finally, a huge banyan tree.

My heart-home is a place
Full of silence-peace.
In front of my heart-home
Are two giant trees:
God's Compassion-Tree
And
God's Forgiveness-Tree.

The Most Important

The body, our outer sheath, is the outer world, and inside the body is the inner world. Inside the body what do we have? The heart. Inside the heart is the soul, and inside the soul is God. God is everywhere, true; but inside the soul, God-Reality is infinitely more manifest, more visible, more tangible. He who embodies the soul-reality consciously, constantly and unconditionally is undoubtedly revealing and manifesting God more than anybody else.

Anything that is more real to us is more important and more meaningful to us. Again, anything that is more important to us becomes more real. God is most important because He is most real; He is the only Reality in His entire universe. At the same time, God is most real to us because He is most important to us.

God is like an expert runner who teaches beginners how to run towards the goal. This moment He is at the goal beckoning to them, the next moment He is at the starting point or in the middle of the course, right beside them. God the Reality is the starting point and God the Reality is the end. But we do not say "end", because God Himself is constantly progressing; He is the ever-transcending Beyond. Today God the Starting Point is our supreme necessity; therefore, the starting point is totally real to us. Tomorrow God the Goal will be our aim, and at that time the goal has to be real to us.

199

The human consciousness once thought that God was unknowable. Now it feels that God is merely unknown. Soon it will realise that God is unmistakably and unreservedly knowable. The divine consciousness knows that there was nothing, there is nothing and there can be nothing other than God.

> *Each human being*
> *Is a special portion*
> *Of the infinite Lord Supreme.*

Loving The Real In Us

I love myself. What do I love about myself? Not my body. If I love my body for the sake of my body, tomorrow I shall be frustrated because there are millions of human beings on earth who are more beautiful than I am. Naturally I will feel miserable. If I love my mind for the sake of my mind, tomorrow I shall see millions of mental giants right in front of me, and my mental capacity will fade into insignificance. If I love my vital dynamism for the sake of my vital dynamism, then I shall see that there are millions of people who are simply inundated with striking dynamism. Similarly, if I love anything else of my own for its own sake, I am bound to be frustrated. I shall defeat my own divine purpose.

If I love myself just because God is expressing Himself through this body, vital, mind, heart and soul, then I see that I am unique and peerless in the whole history of the universe. No other person is going to be created by God with the same capacities, the same understanding, the same experiences. Each individual can love himself just because he is a direct channel of the Divine. God wants to express Himself in each individual in a unique way. When we become consciously and fully one with God, we not only fulfil Him but we also fulfil ourselves.

When we say that we really and truly love ourselves, it means that we consciously feel that Truth is constantly breathing in us, with us and for us. Our very breath on earth is the living reality of Truth. We love and adore ourselves at every moment, not because of our sound bodies, dynamic vitals, refined minds and pure hearts, but because God is inside us, God is utilising us, God is fulfilling Himself in us and through us. Each individual has to be surcharged with this supreme Truth. We should each consciously feel that our life on earth is the outer manifestation of the Supreme's inner Breath. How should we value the inner life? We should value the inner life slowly, steadily, sincerely and devotedly. If we do it in that way, then the inner life is bound to grant us infinite Peace, infinite Light and infinite Bliss.

When you accept the inner life,
Your heart's reality-cry
Must replace your mind's imagination-smile.
What is your heart's reality-cry?
Your heart's reality-cry
Is nothing other than
God's own Transcendental Vision-Smile.

Part Five

The Divine Game

Prayer and Meditation

When I meditate,
My Lord gives me
A heart without walls.
When I pray,
My Lord gives me
A mind with open doors.

I pray. Why do I pray? I pray because I need God. I meditate. Why do I meditate? I meditate because God needs me. When I pray, I think that God is high above me, above my head. When I meditate, I feel that God is deep inside me, inside my heart.

Prayer says, "I am helpless, I am innocent, I am weak. I need You, O Lord Supreme, to strengthen me, to purify me, to illumine me, to perfect me, to immortalise me. I need You, O Lord Supreme."

Meditation says, "Lord Supreme, out of Your infinite Bounty, You have chosen me to be Your instrument to manifest You here on earth in Your own Way. You could have chosen somebody else to play the role, but You have granted me the golden opportunity. To You I offer my constant gratitude, my gratitude-heart."

Prayer is purity. It purifies our mind. The mind is always subject to doubt, fear, worry and anxiety. It is always assailed by wrong thoughts and wrong movements. When we pray, purification takes place in our mind, and purity increases our God-receptivity. In fact, purity is nothing short of God-receptivity. Each time we pray, our inner receptacle becomes large, larger, largest and purity, beauty, light and delight can enter into our receptacle and sport together in the inmost recesses of our heart.

Meditation is luminosity. It illumines our heart. When illumination takes place in our heart, insecurity and the sense of want disappear. At that time we sing the song of inseparable oneness with the Universal and Transcendental Consciousness. When our heart is illumined, the finite in us enters into the Infinite and becomes the Infinite itself. The bondage of millennia leaves us and the freedom of infinite Truth and Light welcomes us.

I pray to God and meditate on God. I pray to God because God is my Lord, my sovereign Lord, my Lord Supreme. I meditate on God because God is my Friend, my eternal Friend, my only Friend.

Just a quick reminder to meditate.
Meditate soulfully;
You will conquer ignorance-night
Easily.
Just a quick reminder to meditate.
Meditate unconditionally;
You will gain the Lord Supreme
Everlastingly.

Medicines For Our Inner Life

Prayer and meditation are medicines to cure us. As we go to a doctor for medicine to cure our physical body, similarly, prayer and meditation are the medicines that will cure us in our inner life.

This is the difference between prayer and meditation. When I pray, I talk and God listens. When I meditate, God talks and I listen. Prayer is important for each individual at the beginning. Meditation comes later. With prayer we grow individually into the highest divinity. But whenever we pray, there is a subtle desire for something. We may call it aspiration, because we pray to become good, to say something good, to do something good, to have something divine which we do not have, or to be free from doubt, jealousy, fear and so on. In meditation we do not do that. We just allow ourselves consciously to enter into the effulgence of light, or we invoke the universal Light to transform our ignorance into wisdom.

Aspiration is within both prayer and meditation. Someone who is praying feels an inner cry to reach God, to realise God. When we pray, we go up, up, up. Someone who is meditating feels the need of bringing God's Consciousness right into his being, into his own consciousness. Aspiration is the only key for both prayer and meditation. Either we reach up to God or He comes down to us. Ultimately, it is the same. God lives on the third floor, but when He comes down to the first floor He is still the same God. One aspirant may go up and get Him; another may bring Him down.

You do not need a cave
To pray to God.
You do not need a forest
To meditate on God.
What you need, you already have
In abundant quality and quantity.
Your loving, self-giving heart
Is all you need,
And you will always have it.

Water The Root

If you wish to help people through your prayers, it is necessary to do a few things first. The most important thing is to meditate or pray every day. You cannot really help people without first getting the inner capacity through your prayer and meditation.

Your prayer and meditation are your inner work. When you work in the morning by praying and meditating, God gives you your salary, your spiritual wealth. Once you have your money, you can give it to others. Your prayers can help another person, but you have to know how. You are praying to God and that particular person has God within him. When you pray for his welfare, you are not touching him directly; you are touching the God in him. Your prayer is going to God, the Source.

What do you do if a plant is dry? You need not actually touch the plant itself. You pour water at the root and the plant again gets strength. As you would go to the root of a plant, go to our Source, who is God. The person you are praying for will get the most benefit if you pray with this idea in mind.

For example, if your father is ill, you have every right to pray to God to cure him, since he is your closest and dearest. You have received affection from him millions of times, and you spontaneously offer your own affection, concern and gratitude in return. This is the human approach to the Supreme. There is tremendous attachment in your concern, because your will has not surrendered to the divine Will.

For the divine approach, you need to add another dimension: "Eternal Father, if it is Your Will, please cure my father." You love your father, so you want him to be cured. But if his cure is not the Will of the Supreme, it is best to let him go when the Supreme wants him to. If you identify your will with the Will of the Supreme, you will see that whether your father stays on earth or not, you will be equally happy, because God's Will will be executed. Without the approval of the Supreme, no human being can die. Even if the dying person is your father, you have to know that he is infinitely dearer to the Supreme than he is to you. The Supreme is our Father and Mother. If one member of the family goes to the father and mother, the other members of the same family will never feel sad.

Prayer-power is incalculable;
It moves mountains easily.
Prayer-glory is ineffable;
It works miracles regularly.

Forms Of Prayer

Prayer will be more effective if you do it on a regular basis. Punctuality is of supreme importance in the prayer-life or the meditation-life. One day you may meditate at six o'clock, one day at seven o'clock, one day at eight o'clock. That is not the right way. You have to be wise. You have to feel there is Somebody who is watching. Nobody is going to stay indefinitely and wait for you to do something good. If you want to do something good, then do it on time.

If your prayer and meditation are informal, this does not mean they are bad. But at the beginning of our spiritual life we will not get intensity from anything that is informal. The forms of ritual will give them a firm foundation to rest on.

Rituals are of supreme necessity in the beginning, because the physical mind has to be convinced. A day will come when it will be fully convinced. Then the seeker will deal directly with the soul and will become part and parcel of the consciousness of the soul. His inner intensity will be spontaneous and constant. If there is intensity, one sees the source and the goal simultaneously. At that time, he will not need any rituals.

I pray
So that I can synchronise
My heart's inner choice
With my life's outer voice.

Guide To Prayer

Straining and praying intensely are two different things. You can pray intensely without straining your nerves. Tremendous intensity can be inside prayer, but intensity is not the same as strain. To eliminate strain while meditating or praying, try to focus all your attention on the heart, not on the mind. First try to see the heart-source. From there you will feel a flow which will be going either upward or downward. Try to direct the flow so it moves upward from the heart. This flow, which is divine Grace, is like water. Each time you pray or meditate, feel that you are digging inside. Naturally, the all-nourishing water comes up, for this water is being supplied constantly from its infinite Source – God.

If you pray with your eyes closed and sometimes drift into sleep for a few seconds, no harm. If you have been praying and meditating for half an hour, then if you sleep for one second, you should feel that you are not actually sleeping, but taking a peaceful rest. But if your prayer is only a short prayer and a long nap, then that kind of prayer is useless. If you have the tendency to fall asleep quite often, then your prayer will be no prayer. In this case, you should pray with your eyes open.

Prayer with words should be outwardly inaudible. Others will not hear it, but you should form a sentence of a few words that will convince the aspiring mind. The heart is already aspiring, but the mind needs to aspire. First, form the sentence by writing it on the tablet of your heart. Then try to see it there. Once the words are written, you can return to see them many times.

We pray and pray
To the soul of the world
To always offer

Its unparalleled assistance
To those who are striving
For a peaceful world.

Concentration

As a general rule, seekers who are just entering the spiritual life should start with concentration for a few months at least. When you concentrate, you become a divine hero. You enter into the arena of life and light where there can be no doubt, no fear. Fear and doubt are conquered by concentration.

Concentration means inner vigilance and alertness. There are thieves all around and within us. Fear, doubt, worry and anxiety are inner thieves that are trying to steal our inner poise and peace of mind. When we learn how to concentrate, it is very difficult for these hostile forces to enter into us. Concentration is the mind's dynamic will that operates in us for our acceptance of light and rejection of darkness. A real aspirant sooner or later acquires the power of concentration either through the Grace of God, through constant practise, or through his own aspiration.

When you concentrate, you are like a bullet entering into something or a magnet pulling the object of concentration towards you. At that time you do not allow any thought to enter into your mind, whether it is divine or undivine, earthly or Heavenly, good or bad. In concentration the entire mind has to be focused on a particular object or subject. If you are concentrating on the petal of a flower, you try to feel that nothing else exists in the entire world but you and the petal. You look neither forward nor backward, upward nor inward; only you try to pierce the object with your one-pointed concentration. But this is not an aggressive way of looking into a thing or entering into an object. Far from it! This concentration comes directly from the soul's indomitable will, or will-power.

Very often I hear aspirants say that they cannot concentrate for more than five minutes. After that they get a headache or their head is on fire. Why? It is because the power of their concentration is coming from the intellectual or disciplined mind. But if the mind is to be utilised properly, then the light of the soul has to enter into it. When the light of the soul has entered into the mind, it is extremely easy to concentrate on something.

As you can concentrate on a flower petal or any other material object, you can also concentrate on your heart. You may close your eyes or look at a wall, but all the time you are thinking of your heart as a dear friend. When this thinking becomes most intense, when it absorbs your entire attention, then you have gone beyond ordinary thinking and entered into concentration. Then gradually the power of your concentration enters into the heart and takes you completely out of the realm of the mind.

Who can overthrow your dreams?
Nobody!
Why?
Because yours are the eyes
That are the daring concentration-spear.

The ABCs Of Meditation

Once you have learned to concentrate, then meditation becomes very easy. But even when you start meditating regularly, it is a good idea to concentrate for a few minutes before you start your daily meditation. If you concentrate, you are like a runner who clears the track of obstacles before he starts to run. Once the track is cleared, you can run very fast.

Let me start with the ABCs of meditation. When you meditate at home, you should have a corner of your room that is absolutely pure and sanctified – a sacred place which you only use for meditation. Here on your shrine you will keep a picture of the Christ, or some other beloved spiritual figure whom you regard as your Master.

When you are doing your daily meditation, try to meditate alone. Collective meditation is also important, but for individual daily meditation it is better to meditate privately at one's own shrine.

Before beginning to meditate, it is helpful if you can take a shower or a bath. If you are unable to do this, you should at least wash your face and your feet. It is also advisable to wear clean and light clothes.

It will help if you burn incense, light a candle and keep some flowers in front of you. There are some people who say that these things are not necessary, but the physical flower that you have in front of you reminds you of the inner flower. The outer flame of the candle makes you feel that the flame in your inner being is also climbing high, higher, highest. When you smell the scent of incense, you get perhaps only an iota of inspiration and purification, but this iota can be added to your inner treasure.

When meditating, it is important to keep the spine straight and erect, and to keep the body relaxed. While you are meditating, your inner being will spontaneously take you to a comfortable position, and then it is up to you to maintain it. The main advantage of the lotus position is that it helps to keep the spinal cord straight and erect. The lotus position is not at all necessary. Many people meditate very well while they are seated in a chair.

If you want a special meditation,
Then to invoke the Presence
Of the Supreme
Is by far the best type of meditation.

The Lion's Meditation

In ninety out of one hundred cases, those who keep their eyes closed during meditation fall asleep. It is best to meditate with the eyes partly open and partly closed. That is called the lion's meditation. Both the physical world, with its noise and distractions, and the subconscious world of sleep are inviting you. You are fighting both of them. Because your eyes are partly open, you will not fall asleep and end up in one of the lower worlds, so you are challenging the world of the subconscious.

At the same time you are maintaining your mastery over the physical plane. If you are having a good meditation with your eyes closed and you feel, say, an insect, you will immediately jump up startled or agitated. But if you keep your eyes open a little, you know that you belong to this world. You are maintaining your poise and inner power here on earth. You can devour any wrong forces around you because you are vigilant, dynamic and alert.

Offering worship to You,
I am so happy,
My Lord.
I am also happy
Because this happiness of mine
Nobody can steal.

Some Breathing Exercises

Proper breathing is very important in meditation. When breathing in, try to breathe as slowly and quietly as possible, so that if someone placed a tiny thread in front of your nose, it would not move at all. And when you breathe out, try to do so even more slowly. If possible,

214

leave a short pause between the end of your exhalation and the beginning of your inhalation. But if it is difficult, do not do it. Never do anything that will harm your organs or respiratory system.

The first thing that you have to think of when breathing is purity. When you breathe in, if you can feel that the breath is coming directly from God, from Purity itself, then your breath can easily be purified.

Then, each time you breathe in, try to feel that you are bringing into your body peace, infinite peace. When you breathe out, feel that you are expelling the restlessness within you and all around you. After practising this a few times, please try to feel that you are breathing in power from the universe. And when you exhale, feel that all your fear is coming out of your body. After doing this a few times, try to feel that what you are breathing in is joy, infinite joy, and what you are breathing out is sorrow, suffering and melancholy.

There is another thing that you can also try. Feel that you are breathing in not air but cosmic energy. Feel that tremendous cosmic energy is entering into you with each breath and that there is not a single place in your body that is not being occupied by the flow of cosmic energy. It is flowing like a river inside you, washing and purifying your whole being. Then when you start to breathe out, feel that you are exhaling all the rubbish inside you – all your undivine thoughts, obscure ideas and impure actions. Anything inside your system that you do not want to claim as your own, feel that you are exhaling.

This is not the traditional yogic *pranayama*, which is more complicated and systematised, but it is the most effective spiritual method of breathing. If you practise it, you will soon see its results. In the beginning you will have to use your imagination, but after a while you will see and feel that it is not imagination at all but reality. You are consciously breathing in the energy that is flowing all around you, purifying yourself and emptying yourself of everything undivine. If you can breathe this way for five minutes every day, you will be able to make very fast progress, but it has to be done in a very conscious way, not mechanically.

Quality, Not Quantity

God-realisation does not depend on how many hours you meditate. It depends on how intensely and deeply you meditate. There are many stories about how aspirants get better results when they meditate soulfully and are not concerned about the number of hours. I wish to tell one story:

Narada was a great singer and a great devotee of the god Vishnu. Once he became bloated with pride because he was Vishnu's dearest devotee. Lord Vishnu wanted to smash his pride, so one day he said to Narada, "I want you to go into the world and visit my dearest disciple on earth."

Narada could not say it out loud to his Master, but inwardly he felt, "Your dearest disciple on earth? Who is it? Who could be dearer than I?"

Vishnu said, "In a certain village there is a man who is a farmer, and this farmer is extremely devoted to me. I want you to go and visit him."

Narada went to the farmer's house and stayed there for a few days. The farmer had a big family, with children and grandchildren. He shouldered heavy responsibilities, but early in the morning, before he went to cultivate the land, he uttered the name of Lord Vishnu three times most soulfully. Narada followed him into the field, and saw that at noon again he uttered the name of Lord Vishnu three times most soulfully. When he came back home he repeated Vishnu's name three times more, and then he entered into his household affairs. For two or three days Narada observed the spirituality and daily meditation of the farmer.

Narada came back to Vishnu and said, "How can you say that that farmer is your dearest disciple? He repeats your name only three times in the morning, three times at noon, and three times at night. I repeat your name thousands and thousands of times during the day, and I have been doing it for so many years! How many years I have been praying to you, meditating on you and chanting your name to inspire people!"

Vishnu said, "Wonderful, Narada. Now, I am thirsty. Please bring me a glass of water from the nearest pond."

Narada went to fetch water for Vishnu, and there in the pond he saw a beautiful girl swimming. He fell in love with the girl and forgot to bring water for his Master. He married the girl and started a new life. They had a few children, and in this way many years passed. Then there was a famine in the place where Narada was living and all his children died, and his wife died also. He was crying to relieve his suffering, "O Lord Vishnu, save, me, save me!"

Vishnu came to him and said, "What about my glass of water?" and brought him back to reality.

Vishnu said, "It is just a minor thing to bring me a glass of water. But in the world of ignorance and illusion you lost all your devotion, aspiration, spirituality, everything. Now look at this farmer. He has such a big family, every day he is shouldering such heavy responsibilities, but even then he has the time to think of me, to meditate on me. I gave him his work of cultivating the fields; I gave him the responsibility of supporting a family. He discharges all his family responsibilities, but still he has time to think of me and meditate on me. But when I gave you something to do, you immediately forgot me."

There are some people who make the complaint that they have no time to meditate because they are working so hard. They are fooling themselves. If you are really working hard, divinely and supremely, then God will give you time. And if you are working with utmost devotion, inside that devoted service you are getting the benefit of meditation. From this story we come to realise that it is not how many hours you meditate but how soulfully you meditate that is important. I wish to say that if an aspirant is really intense, if God comes first in his life, then he can easily adjust his outer life to make time to meditate. The inner aspiration has infinitely more power than the outer obstacles. If you utilise your inner strength, then the circumstances have to surrender to your inner aspiration. Outer obstacles can easily be overcome because the inner life is the living expression of infinite Power.

Not enough, not enough,
If the spirituality-lesson
Is merely learned
From books and philosophers.
It must be translated
Into regular practise,
It must be lived
In its pristine form.

In The Divine Flow

We can experience true meditation when we are consciously aware of the Supreme. We have to know that it is He who is fulfilling Himself in and through us, that He is doing the meditation Himself. We are just the vessel and we are allowing Him to fill us with His whole Consciousness. When we are aware of this, after five or ten minutes of meditation we will enter into the very world of meditation. We do not have to do anything; we are there in that world because the Supreme has taken charge of our meditation.

We start with our own physical and mental effort, but once we go deep within we see that it is not effort that allows us to enter into meditation. Meditation will be complicated so long as we depend on ourselves. But when we feel that meditation is being done by the Supreme in us with our conscious awareness and consent, then meditation cannot be complicated. At that time we will see that our meditation is free and spontaneous. God is fulfilling Himself through us, and enlarging His Consciousness within us. But it has to be done with our consent.

When you meditate, please try to feel the river of meditation flowing through you without coercion or exertion. Let the divine Consciousness flow through you. That flow is the real meditation. Then, if you want to increase your receptivity, each day before you meditate, offer your deepest gratitude to the Supreme. This is the easiest and most effective way to increase receptivity. Because you are aspiring, you have become something. Then tomorrow, if you have maintained your aspiration, you will go one step further.

Each time you offer gratitude, you again go forward. And when you go forward, automatically your receptivity increases. Receptivity means what? It means progress. The more you receive, the more you can make progress in the inner world. Again, the more you receive, the more you have the capacity to receive.

> God's Compassion exists
> In every life-experience of yours,
> Whether you believe it or not.

Meditation-Meals

Sometimes you do not feel like eating, but you know that the body needs food, so you still eat every day. It is a natural habit, the body's demand. Similarly, even if you cannot meditate properly or have your best meditation every day, you should not be worried.

In order to maintain the same level of meditation, you have to be very spiritually advanced. I am not throwing cold water on your efforts; far from it. I wish to say that in the beginning you should be happy if, even occasionally, you get a very good, very high, sublime meditation. When you do not have a good meditation, do not allow yourself to become a victim of frustration. If you become frustrated, you will lose your capacity to an even greater extent. Then on the following day, it will also be impossible for you to meditate deeply.

Here you have to realise that you are not an expert in meditation. Now your meditation is at the mercy of your inspiration or aspiration. How can we become an expert in anything? If we want to be a singer or a poet or a dancer, we have to practise daily. It is the same with meditation. When we practise meditation daily, there comes a time when it becomes spontaneous. If we do not feed the soul, our inner being, every day, then the soul or the aspirant in us starves. And what happens then? We cannot reveal, we cannot manifest our own divinity.

In the spiritual life
Everything you do
Is important.
Every second of your life
Is supremely important.

One Step At A Time

When we start something for the first time, we get inspiration. But if we continue doing it, we do not have the same enthusiasm, the same impetus. We want to get something very deep, high and sublime, something most illumining from our daily meditation. We are like a long-distance runner. When the starter fires the gun, at the very beginning he is really inspired and he starts running very fast. After about two or three miles, he becomes tired; running becomes tedious and difficult. Now if he gives up running just because he is tired and his inspiration is gone, he does not reach the goal. But if he continues running, he will finally reach it. Then he will definitely feel that it was worth the struggle and the suffering of the body.

It is like that in the spiritual life also. When you start your meditation-journey in the morning, feel that it is a continuation of your previous day's meditation. Do not take it as a new beginning. Every day feel that you have travelled another mile. The day you start your spiritual journey is actually the most important. At that time you will have the most inspiration. But if you can feel that each morning during your meditation you are travelling a little farther, you will know that one day you will reach your Goal. Even if your speed decreases, you have to continue running and not give up on the way. When you reach the Goal, you will see that it was worth the struggle.

To see God the Light,
To feel God the Light,
To become God the Light:
This is the only goal
Of my meditation.

Manifestation

Whenever we see
From God's point of view,
We feel this world
Is full of God-Light-manifestation.

My philosophy is the absolute acceptance of life. In this life there is the living Breath of God. If we really think of God, if we feel His existence, then we have to accept the world as real, just as God is real. God and His creation can never be separated.

There have been spiritual Masters who negated the world, who did not care for it. They wanted their own self-realisation and when they got it they said goodbye to the world. Then again, there are many spiritual Masters who have accepted life. They said, "The world is within me. Unless and until the world is perfected, how can I be perfect?" Now if you say that those who are isolated, those who enter into the Himalayan caves and neglect society, will find less difficulty in realising God, granted. But if they do not accept humanity, what do they ultimately gain? If your plot of land is tiny, only one acre, then your crop will also be tiny. But if you have much land and the materials and capacity to cultivate it, then you are bound to get a bumper crop. In the same way, you are bound to get a bumper crop of realisation in infinite measure because you have accepted humanity.

If I love my Father, and if I see that my brothers and sisters have not yet realised Him, then what will I do? I will give my light, my achievement, to them. That the world has to be relinquished – this is an old Indian theory which is absolutely wrong. Today you will renounce the world, tomorrow you will renounce your family members and the day after tomorrow you will renounce yourself. Then what are you going to do?

The path of world-acceptance is undoubtedly the path of heroes. We have to fight against doubt, worry, fear, obstruction, limitation, imperfection, bondage and death. But if we really love God, then nothing is difficult. Everything becomes very secure and safe. This is the easiest and most fulfilling path for the sincere, for the totally dedicated, for the brave souls who are ready to walk, march, run and fly along the path of Eternity.

> *Our soul encourages*
> *And inspires us*
> *To run towards God*
> *With lightning speed.*

The Body As A Conscious Instrument

Man is God yet to be supremely realised in the highest plane of consciousness, and God is man yet to be totally manifested and fulfilled here on earth. Each individual represents God. Your concept of God may be that He is unlimited, but He is also deep inside you. If you go deep within, you will see that inside your body is God. Then as you go deeper still, you will see that your outer body is also God. You have to see with a different eye, not with your physical eyes. When you approach Truth with your aspiration, with your soul's inner urge, you see that God is everywhere. He is inside you. He is also in an insect, in a cloud, in a tree, in energy. I am God; you are God; we are all God. God is omniscient, omnipotent and omnipresent, but He must be manifested and fulfilled on earth. That is why we are here.

We need the body, the physical, for manifestation. The soul may realise something here on earth, but manifestation requires the body. Let us compare the spiritual life to a university, where we learn many things. If there is no house, no room, no hall, where are we going to give a lecture? Everything needs outer protection. If we do not have a house, where will we live? In the street? No, we will be blown away. Similarly, we need a body in order to house the eternal wealth within us. The soul makes us aware of the inner wealth when we concentrate and meditate. Then it gives us the capacity to reveal the inner light to the world at large. While revealing, we are manifesting the divinity within us.

You have to feel that the body is a divine instrument. It is not only the heart or the soul that will work for God. The physical also has to work. If you bake a cake, if you work at a printing press, if you do any service on the physical plane, feel that the inspiration comes directly from God and you are just executing it. You have to keep in mind that this body is the instrument of manifestation. If you keep the instrument in good condition, then only can the player play. If you neglect the body, then how can the divine Player, God, use the body in His cosmic Game?

This body will one day become a conscious instrument. Now the body does not always listen to the dictates of the soul. The physical mind at times revolts. On very rare occasions it listens to the soul. Even when we hear the message from our soul, we may not do the right thing. But a day will come when the soul is in a position to exercise its divine qualities. When the physical, vital and mind want to listen to the soul, want to be instructed and guided by the soul, then here in the physical we will have a divinised consciousness. It may take time for the physical to be transformed, but it has to be totally transformed. Here on earth God feels that His Absolute Manifestation must take place; for that He needs the outer structure, and the body plays this role.

The wish of my soul:
My body will become
A perfect instrument of God.
The wish of my body:
My soul will be
My body's ever-leading
And ever-forgiving captain.

Physical Strength Versus Spiritual Strength

It is true that the body has to be a perfect instrument of the spirit. But we have to know that it need not be a perfect body. The world's best athletes are not necessarily manifesting the divine Will unless they are conscious instruments of the Supreme. Physical perfection does not necessarily indicate receptivity to the light of the spirit. The message of the soul, our heart's inner cry for God, for Truth, for light – these things are not connected at all with bodily strength. We become aware of our inner, spiritual life only through prayer and meditation.

If you compare the physical strength of any of the world's greatest spiritual Masters with that of the world's greatest boxers or wrestlers, the spiritual Masters are nowhere. But if any of these Masters with his spiritual strength were to challenge a fighter, then that fighter would be compelled to surrender. Physical strength is nothing in comparison to spiritual strength.

The body needs strength so that it can receive and manifest the message of the spirit. If matter is not strong or receptive, then how can the message of the spirit be manifested in the physical? Suppose we want to meditate in the morning. If we are physically weak, if we have a stomach ache or headache or some other ailment, then how will we meditate well? That is why we have to give due importance to the body; but due importance does not mean extravagant concern.

If our body is strong enough and healthy enough to perform its natural functions, and if it is capable of sitting quietly for two or three hours without any difficulty or unusual discomfort, that is more than enough. The body has to be a fit instrument, but that does not mean we have to become the strongest or the most powerful person. It is sufficient to have the amount of strength that our body requires in order to stay on earth and play our God-ordained role efficiently.

> *Be Thou my body*
> *That I may wake.*
> *Be Thou my vital*
> *That I may run.*
> *Be Thou my mind*
> *That I may fly.*
> *Be Thou my heart*
> *That I may dive.*
> *Be Thou my soul*
> *That I may reveal.*
> *Be Thou my Goal*
> *That I may fulfil.*
> *Be Thou my All*
> *That I may only be Yours.*

Realisation And Manifestation

We are one with the Self, but we are not now aware of it. We can be aware of it only when we consciously practise spirituality, and for that we need aspiration. When we are marching along the path of aspiration, our spirit will automatically blend with our physical being, and the physical being will devotedly listen to the dictates of the Self. Then we will see that our inner life and outer life have become totally one. At that time, one complements and fulfils the other. The inner life becomes the embodiment of the Truth and the outer life becomes the manifestation of the Truth.

In our meditation we realise and in our dedication we manifest. When we meditate, we try to realise the Truth, and when we dedicate ourselves to work in the world, we try to manifest the realisation that we achieved during our meditation.

When you eat, you enter into the world of food and get the realisation of food; you get its strength. Then, the next moment, what do you do? You go to your shop or office and work. First you identify yourself with something powerful; then you manifest it. When your body is weak, you cannot do any work. When you enter into the world of food, that means that you are entering into the world of dynamic power. Then you manifest this power through work. Realisation and manifestation have to go together.

Early in the morning, when you meditate, you enter into the spiritual plane, where there is peace, light and bliss. That is realisation. Then you have to offer it to your spiritual brothers and sisters. That is manifestation. When you are eating, you are realising the food-power. When you are meditating, you are realising the spiritual power. Then, the next moment, you will talk to someone and he will see in you something sweet, something divine, something kind. Is this not the manifestation of the realisation that you had early in the morning while you were praying to the Supreme?

If you do not bring your divine qualities forward and offer them to humanity, how can you be satisfied? It is like material wealth. If you do not bring the money out of your pocket, then how are you going to buy anything or achieve anything? It is impossible. All divine qualities you have, but you have to bring them forward.

When your good qualities
Go and touch others,
Their good qualities come forward
To receive from you.

Pieces Of Mango

Through realisation, manifestation must come. Inside your pocket is a most delicious mango. You put your hand inside the pocket and bring out the mango and show it to me. This is revelation. Before, the mango was concealed, and now you have revealed it. Then you have to manifest it. How will you do that? You will cut it into a few pieces and share it with me and with others.

When you reveal God or Truth or Light to the world, it means that you have brought these things forward and they are there for all the world to see. But if nobody looks at what you have revealed, or if nobody accepts or understands it, then this is revelation without manifestation. Take realisation as something inside you. Manifest it here on earth; then it becomes the possession of others. When you reveal it, others become aware of it, but still your Truth does not become their possession. But when you manifest it, your Truth becomes the possession of the entire world. That is why I give so much importance to manifestation.

Each soul has come into the world
For the full manifestation
Of God's Delight-Dream
On earth.

The Potter's Clay

The universe is God's manifestation, but it is not yet God's perfection. Through the process of evolution, God is proceeding toward His Self-perfection. Divine perfection is the gradual transformation of our entire being, of our entire consciousness. Spirit has descended into matter. Now, with aspiration, Spirit has to return to its highest sphere.

In the outer world we may see limitation, imperfection, doubt, fear and death. But in the inner world we see light, peace, bliss and perfection. When we live in God's Consciousness, there is no imperfection. What actually exists is consciousness on various levels, enjoying itself in its various manifestations. In the field of manifestation, consciousness has different grades. Why do we pray and meditate? Because this leads us from a lower degree of illumination to a higher degree, because it brings us closer to something pure, beautiful, inspiring and fulfilling. The highest illumination is God-realisation. This illumination must take place not only in the soul, but also in the heart, mind, vital and body.

If we ignore manifestation, if we ignore the everyday world, we will be living in a dream world. First we have to accept the world as it is. If we do not accept the world, then what are we going to transform? If a potter does not accept his clay, then how is he going to shape and mould a pot? We have to aspire to bring down peace, light and bliss for the world. We have to enter into the very breath of life in humanity in order to transform and change the face of the earth. The material life and the spiritual life must run together. We have to both accept the world as it is and to work and work to raise the earth-consciousness, to free it from limitations, imperfections, bondage and ignorance.

He who is reluctant
To break stones
Will never be able to become
A path-maker.

The Connecting Link

We want to love the world; we want to fulfil the world. But sometimes we may feel there is no connecting link – that our existence and the world's existence are two totally different things. In this we are making a deplorable mistake. What is the proper connecting link between us and the world? God.

We can serve the Supreme in others; but why use the term "in others"? If we remain in the heart, then we will never speak of serving the Supreme in others. We will speak of serving Him in ourselves, in our own aspiring consciousness. Right now we are still wanting in oneness. As long as there is a sense of separateness, we need to acquire more aspiration before we can feel that there is somebody else whom we have to accept as our own.

When I am in the desire-world, I need only my own fulfilment. Then there comes a time when I have to admit that you also exist. When I have accepted your existence, what still remains to be realised is our oneness. First I have a sense of separateness. Although I, as an individual, am the body, vital, mind, heart and soul, and you, as an individual, are the same, I still find it difficult to claim you or to see you as my own. There has to be a connecting link, and this is the Source, the Supreme.

When we aspire, we come to realise that we have a Source and that others also have the same Source. If we do not know who He is, then it will be simply impossible for us to feel united with Him. Right now we need somebody to connect us. As long as I know that both you and I are His creation, I can invoke the Creator to make us inseparably one. Only the mind is not allowing us to feel that we are the self-same reality. The mental world will always offer the message of separateness, whereas the psychic world will always offer us the message of oneness, inseparable oneness.

If we are in the heart
Of God-consciousness,
Then we are definitely
Lifting up
The burden of the world.

Swami Vivekananda's Heart Of Oneness

Swami Vivekananda, the great disciple of Sri Ramakrishna Paramahansa, looked upon the world as his dear motherland, and upon mankind as his true brothers and sisters. Come what may, to serve them was his cherished religion. "Better to wear out than to rust out" – Vivekananda's life vibrated with this unique idea. His was a life of unimaginable sacrifice.

After speaking at the Parliament of Religions in Chicago in 1893, Swami Vivekananda became famous overnight and acquired many friends and admirers. One day some of these people came to ask him many questions about Vedanta, Indian philosophy and spirituality. They were very moved by his answers. By the time they departed, it was around midnight.

All of a sudden Vivekananda thought of India, especially his home, Mother Bengal. He said to himself, "Now I am going to bed. But there are thousands and thousands of people without beds, who will be lying in the street, poverty-stricken, tonight. Here I have got a cosy and most comfortable bed. But once upon a time I was a *sannyasin*, a wandering monk. I used to roam in the street with no food, nothing. Even now I am a *sannyasin*.

"Again, God blesses me with riches and my generous friends keep me in their homes. Right now some friends of mine have given me this beautiful apartment. Indeed, I am in great luxury. And yet so many of my brothers and sisters in Bengal are living in the street. My heart bleeds for them. I have still not fulfilled my task. I have to help them, I have to awaken their consciousness. There is so much to do, so much to do! Alas, what am I doing here? I need rest, but I will not sleep on the bed. I will sleep on the floor."

He took off his turban, placed it on the floor and passed the night sleeping on the floor. Early the following morning, when his friend, the owner of the apartment, came to invite him to breakfast, he saw this Indian saint, this great hero, lying on the floor. He said, "What is the matter?"

Vivekananda replied, "Thousands and thousands of my brothers and sisters spend the night in the streets, so how can I dream of spending the night in this most comfortable bed? I cannot, I cannot, unless and until I have done something for them. It is my bounden duty to serve God in the poor and the needy. The life of comfort is not for me. The life of selfless, dedicated, devoted service is for me. Service is my goal; service is my perfection in life."

O let my heart sow!
Let others' lives reap!

Inspiring Others

If you are aspiring, you need not reach the Highest in order to help other aspiring people. If you give according to your capacity, God is satisfied. He knows the amount of peace, light and bliss He has given you. If you distribute that, then He will definitely give you more next time. You will never run short. The amount that you receive and give may not be according to your mind's satisfaction, but God sees your capacity and how much your vessel can hold. As it expands, naturally He will be able to pour in more peace and light. Only then will you be able to offer more to others.

You also cannot go in the street and tell everyone, "I have peace, light and bliss. Just come and take it from me." If you say that, others will just laugh at you. If you speak about your inner experiences, you may run into difficulty. The soil has to be fertile. Only if people are genuine and sincere, will your conversation be fruitful.

If you give a hundred-dollar bill to a child, he will tear it up. For him there is no value in it. But a grown-up will know the value of a hundred dollars. Similarly, when you share your inner experiences with an aspirant or seeker, he will benefit by it. He knows how difficult it is to have an inner experience. Those who really cry for the inner life are the right persons to share your experiences with.

The most effective way to inspire others is to become aspiration itself. You may not be flooded with aspiration all the time, but you do have a certain amount of it because you are practising the spiritual life and because you are trying soulfully to receive peace, light and bliss in abundant measure. If you become the embodiment of aspiration, then automatically others will become inspired.

Try not to put others right;
That is God's task.
Try to put yourself right;
Indeed, that is your
God-ordained task.

The Dream Of The Soul

This world is the field of manifestation where we can manifest our inner divine qualities. The soul is playing a game, and that game is called the game of manifestation. We have to make ourselves feel that the manifestation of the dream of the soul is the only thing that we need. The dream of the soul is our treasured breath, and the manifestation of this dream is our only goal. If we have that kind of inner awareness, then at every moment we can be sincere to our soul's need and the soul's immortal reality.

There is no end to our aspiration. In the beginning when we aspire, deep within us we feel that we have to realise God. Then we have to feel the necessity of revealing God to humanity. This again is aspiration, on a higher level. After we have revealed God, we have to manifest God. This is the third step. Manifestation is the flowering of real aspiration. But there is no end to our manifestation, just as there is no end to our realisation and no end to our revelation. Each realisation of today is tomorrow's starting point, tomorrow's new dawn.

May each dream of our soul
Find its complete fulfilment
On earth.

The Path of the Divine Hero

Mine is not the way
To follow the world.
Mine is not the way
To lead the world.
Mine is the way
To walk along with God.

We came from the Blissful. To the Blissful we shall return with the spontaneous joy of life. It is a mistaken idea that the spiritual life is a life of austerity and a bed of thorns. It seems difficult because we cater to our ego. It looks unnatural because we cherish our doubts.

We all, with no exception, have the power of self-realisation or God-realisation. The realisation of God is, indeed, the goal of our life. What we have to do is accept life and fulfil the Divine in ourselves here on earth. This we can do only by transcending our human limitations.

God is at once our Father and Mother. As our Father, He observes; as our Mother, She creates. Like a child, we shall never give up demanding of our Mother, so that we can win our Mother's Love and Grace. How long can a mother go without heeding her child's cry? Let us not forget that if there is anybody on whom all human beings have a full claim, it is the Mother aspect of the Divine. She is the only strength of our dependence. She is the only strength of our independence. Her Heart, the home of infinitude, is eternally open to each individual.

235

Today You have given me
The message of surrender.
I have offered to You
My very flower-heart.
In the dark night with tears,
In the unknown prison-cell of illusion,
In the house of the finite,
No longer shall I abide.
I know You are mine.
I have known this, Mother,
O Queen of the Eternal.

Achieving The Goal

There is great joy in achieving something, doing something and becoming something. If we can do the most difficult things, naturally we can achieve the most, offer the most and become the most. The easiest thing on earth is to become jealous of somebody, to feel insecure or depressed, to become proud or undivine. But to see God inside someone else is a most difficult thing. The easiest thing everybody can do and almost everybody does, but how many people are doing or have done the most difficult thing? You are wise enough to know the value of God-realisation, the most difficult thing to do.

To realise God is like completing the 400-metre dash. Whereas, to act undivinely or to harbour undivine qualities is like running one metre: the moment you start your journey, you reach your goal. If you continue running in the 400-metre dash, then immediately one metre goes away, then two, then three, four, five and so on, until you reach your goal. On your way, you leave behind the first metre, which was your jealousy. You leave behind the second metre, which was perhaps your insecurity. You leave behind the third metre, which was perhaps your pride and vanity, and so on. The moment you reach your goal and become one with your goal, all the metres that you covered on your way are far behind you.

The problem with many seekers is that although they have started their journey, they do not feel the necessity of reaching the goal. They are just taking a morning walk and enjoying fresh air. Only if you feel the necessity of arriving at the goal will you be constantly and dynamically on the move. The goal is four hundred metres away, but after covering one metre if you feel afraid that you will not reach the goal, if you feel that it is quite far away and you decide to give up, then next week or next year, when you want to run again, you have to start back where you began.

In the spiritual life also, if you stop your journey for some time because of jealousy, insecurity or any other undivine reason, ignorance pulls you so hard that you go back farther than your original starting point.

But shall we surrender to ignorance? No! Because of our wisdom, we want God, only God; we want Light, only Light. If we can increase our love of God, then we can easily overcome the ignorance-power that is attacking us.

Now, how can you increase your love of God? Every morning feel that you are a newly blossomed flower in God's Heart-Garden. And who is the Gardener? It is God Himself. As the Creator, He Himself creates you as a flower; and again, as the Gardener, He breathes in the beauty and smells the fragrance of His creation. Then He gets tremendous joy.

Beyond speech and mind,
Into the river of ever-effulgent Light
My heart dives.
Today thousands of doors,
Closed for millennia,
Are opened wide.

Ignorance Versus God's Grace

Ignorance may be trying to catch us, but we are running away at the fastest speed. We are running towards our goal. The goal of ignorance-power is to grab us, but before it grabs us, we run so fast towards our destination that ignorance cannot catch us.

It is true that we run faster if there are no obstacles or impediments in our way, but if there are impediments, each time we cross one hurdle we get additional strength and encouragement to try to cross another one. If we have no hurdles, we are fortunate. But if we do have some, because of our long association with ignorance, we should feel confident that we will be able to transcend them because we have aspiration, the inner impetus to pass all obstacles and reach the Goal.

If we go deep within, we can see each difficulty as a boon. Formerly we were alone with our difficulties. Now we have become conscious aspirants, so God's Grace has entered into our lives. God's Grace is constantly helping the seeker. It stands between the difficulty and the seeker. If we see millions of difficulties when we sincerely enter into the spiritual life, then we can also see them as millions of blessings, because God's Grace is in them, illumining them. The sooner difficulties appear before us the better, because then we can surmount them.

There are two ways to make yourself happy. One way is to run and hide. The other way is to act like a roaring lion and fight. If undivine forces have entered into you, do not be disturbed, do not feel that you are helpless. Feel that some forces have attacked you; now you have to fight back with your peace, light and bliss.

But what if you do not have peace, light and bliss at that time because you did not aspire that day? You can remember that you did aspire yesterday, or the previous day, or a few days before. When you are attacked, think of your previous achievement. Today you are beginning to doubt and cherish negative forces, but perhaps yesterday you had a good meditation. Immediately try to think of that meditation and bring it into your living memory. Then your spiritual power will automatically come to the fore.

You are not fooling yourself; the divine experiences of yesterday are your real wealth. Yesterday you had the highest experience or you received more light. Always try to think of one good past experience. This good, high experience was a reality. Today's attack is also a form of reality. Do not allow yourself to be mercilessly attacked and destroyed by today's reality.

> *We will never limit ourselves*
> *If we can feel*
> *That there is Somebody deep within us*
> *To inspire us, to guide us,*
> *To mould us, to shape us*
> *And to take us*
> *On an endless journey*
> *To an ever-transcending Reality.*

Will-Power

In the spiritual life, we are all divine heroes. At every moment we are struggling against our enemies. What is our weapon? Aspiration. Along with aspiration, we have to have will-power, which is of paramount importance.

When we see a person of determined will, we may feel that he has no humility, that he is arrogant, egotistic or autocratic. We may feel that humility and determination are poles apart, but this is only because we do not understand the meaning of humility. When we use the term humility, we often feel that somebody has been humiliated by someone else. On the contrary, true humility is the feeling of sweetest oneness. If we are humble, the whole world feels that we have the willingness or receptivity to hold it within our own heart even though it has countless undivine qualities. In divine humility we can see a true determination that is founded upon simplicity, sincerity and purity.

The quality that we call determination in our day-to-day life is called will-power in the inner world. Real will-power comes from the inmost recesses of our heart, where the soul is located. It is not the product of the mind; it comes directly from the soul. The soul's light operates in our outer life as will-power to achieve or manifest something on earth.

What else can will-power do? It can enter into the divine Reality sooner than at once. We knock at the door of Reality with our sincerity, purity, aspiration, dedication and devotion, but it may take a few days or months before this door actually opens for us. When divine determination, divine will-power, knocks at the door of Reality, immediately the door opens wide. Why? Because Reality sees two things at once. It sees that will-power has the capacity to embody it, whereas other qualities may not have the necessary strength to immediately embody Reality when it is thrust upon them. Reality also sees that when it wants to manifest itself on earth, it is human will-power which takes up the challenge to help.

No matter how feeble our will-power is in comparison to God's adamantine Will, human will-power will say, "God, I am ready to fulfil You. I want to be Your instrument, I want to be Your dynamic hero. My power may be limited, but this limited quantity I am ready to use. Do You want to sit on my shoulder? Then sit. Do You want me to run for You? Then I will run." This determination, this will-power, is never afraid of saying or doing anything. It knows that its strength comes forth from the soul, and that the soul has God as its very own.

God's Will does everything, provided you know what Grace is and what its capacity is. Otherwise you will say, "If I meditate for five hours, God's Grace will descend like a drop of honey." A drop of honey is sweet, but will it have power in your life? You have to feel that Grace itself is omnipotent Power; only then will you be able to know that it will be able to conquer your weaknesses. You have to feel that God's Compassion is something infinitely stronger than the undivine force that is attacking you. Then you will see what Grace can do; you will see that God's Grace is fighting on your side most powerfully.

Be not afraid of the impossible.
Be brave!
God is always ready to help you
Conquer the impossible.

One Less Rascal On Earth

Thomas Carlyle says, "Try to make yourself honest. If you become honest, then rest assured that there will be one less rascal in the world." If one person becomes perfect, there will be one less imperfect person on earth. If I value my inner strength and if I want to get rid of my weaknesses, who can prevent me? Let us say that one room is in darkness because there is no electricity, while another room has light. I can go into the room that has light. Who can prevent me? Who is asking me not to go there? Again, if I bring an electrician into the room that is unlit, then in a few minutes there will be light in that room.

There is light, and there is infinite Light. Let us say that inside weakness also there is light. Inside everything that God has created, even inside darkness, there is light. But if I see the dark sky and the effulgent sun side by side, will I not go to the sun? Will I go to the inferior light? If I am wise, I will always go to the side that is bright, brighter, brightest. I will not go to the darker side. Why should I go there? If I go to the darkness, then I will be destroyed. I am the one who has to observe which side is most beautiful and most powerful. The other side may be pretending to be most beautiful, but my heart will tell me which side is real, which side is infinitely stronger and more beautiful. I shall always choose the real strength, and that real strength is constant, sleepless and breathless love of God.

God's miraculous achievement:
I truly love Him.

Always Use The Heart

Always use the heart. The heart is always carrying newness, whereas the mind is carrying oldness. By the second day, the mind loses all enthusiasm because it feels that everything is too old, but for the heart, every day is new, like the sun. When the sun rises, the mind will not care to look at the sun, because the mind feels that it is the same old sun. Whether the sun is coming out of the water or out of the clouds, the mind does not care. But the heart is waiting for the sun. The heart says, "When will it come? When will it come? When will it come?" If we use the heart to obey God, to please God, then everything is new. Every day, even though we are doing and seeing the same things outwardly, the heart is constantly feeling new joy.

When you offer your gratitude-heart, then it expands; and when it expands it becomes one with God's Universal Reality. Early in the morning, before you meditate or do anything, offer as much gratitude as possible; offer your soulful tears just because you have become what you are now. If you do this, eventually you will become infinitely more than what you are now. Gratitude will be able to make you feel what God's Will is. If you offer gratitude, God's Will will act in and through you and God will do everything in and through you.

God gave me something special:
Awareness.
I gave God something special:
Willingness.
Now God wants to give me
His Satisfaction
And I want to give God
My gratitude.

Arise, Awake, Aspire!

When we go deep within, we see that one who chooses the Supreme has already been chosen by the Supreme. It is God who has chosen each of us before we even dreamt of accepting Him as our very own. But now that we are consciously aware of His acceptance, we need not stumble, we need not walk, we need not march; we can run fast, faster, fastest, because our awareness is already God's infinite Grace.

Millions of people are fast asleep in the world of ignorance, whereas we are fortunate enough to have been aroused by the Supreme Himself. He has said to us, "Arise, awake, aspire!" We have risen. We are now awakened. We are now aspiring. The mounting flame of consciousness deep within us is climbing towards the highest. Arise, awake, aspire! These three soul-stirring words at every moment we shall cherish.

Where is our Goal? It is not in the blue skies, it is not in the vast ocean, it is not in the distant desert – it is deep inside us, in the inmost recesses of our heart. Our spiritual heart is infinitely larger than the world. The world grows and flows inside the spiritual heart. If we can feel that our aspiring heart is the living breath of the Supreme, then we are bound to feel that our cherished goal is within, not without.

243

In order to realise the Goal, to reach the Goal deep within, we have to renew our life and make it fresh every day. Each day early in the morning we have to revitalise our outer life with golden hope. This hope is not an idle dream; it is the precursor of the divinity that will manifest in and through our outer nature. It is our dynamic divine quality that sees the Beyond even when it is still a far cry.

Break asunder all my hopes.
Only keep one hope,
And that hope is to learn
The language of Your inner Silence
In my utter unconditional surrender.
In Your clear and free Sky
I shall be calm and perfect.
The bird of my heart is dancing today
In the festival of supernal Light.

The Process Of Perfection

Perfect perfection here on earth has to be manifested, but how? We have to start our journey with inspiration. We have to feel every day deep within us in all our activities, the necessity of inspiration. Without it there can be no proper achievement.

Then we have to go one step further: we have to feel the momentous necessity of aspiration. We have to aspire to reach the Golden All, to see the Golden Shore of the Beyond. This is what we expect from aspiration, the mounting flame within us.

But aspiration is not enough either. We have to meditate. Aspiration includes meditation. When we meditate, we have to feel that we are entering into Infinity, Eternity and Immortality. These are not vague terms, but our true possessions. To someday enter into our own divine possessions is our birthright.

When we become advanced in our meditation, when it starts offering us its fruit, we enter the realm of realisation. We realise the highest Truth in this body, here on earth. We do not have to go elsewhere to realise God. We do not have to enter an Himalayan cave or sit on a snow-capped mountain in order to practise spirituality. Here on earth, in the hustle and bustle of life, we have to practise our spiritual life. We have to accept earth as it stands, as it is. If we are afraid of earth, then God-realisation will always remain a far cry.

But even realisation is not enough. We have to reveal our realisation, not act like a miser, hoarding our treasure. We have to offer to the world our realisation in the form of revelation.

Yet revelation is not enough either. We have to enter into the domain of manifestation. If we do not manifest what we have realised, we can never be truly fulfilled. Mother Earth has to be fed with the fruit of our realisation. Here on earth the manifestation of realisation has to take place, and when it does, perfection is bound to dawn. Perfect perfection is nothing other than the absolute manifestation of God's transcendental Will here on earth.

I shall listen to Your Command, I shall.
In Your Sky I shall fly, I shall fly.
Eternally You are mine, my very own.
You are my heart's wealth.
For You at night in tears I shall cry.
For You at dawn with light I shall smile.
For You, for You, Beloved, only for You.